Acclaim for Kate Braestrup's

MARRIAGE
and
OTHER ACTS
of
CHARITY

"An insightful look at the role marriage and loving relationships of every sort play in everyday lives....Braestrup is self-deprecating, funny and feisty, and seemingly extremely honest with herself. She writes of her religion and its teachings in an approachable way, much like spiritual author Anne Lamott....Many readers will wish Braestrup were the minister of their local church."
—Amy Canfield, *Miami Herald*

"Braestrup has survived tragedy (the death of her first husband, chronicled in *Here If You Need Me*) and regularly stands witness to the sorrows of others. Through it all, she keeps her feet on the ground and her faith and humor intact. She uses real-life stories to contemplate love, loss, and religion, and by sharing her struggle toward understanding, she lights the way for us....Braestrup's book asks us to stay open to grace." —Anne Leslie, *People*

"An inspirational book that's both religious and secular, that's serious, funny, and smart." —Joan Silverman, *Portland Press Herald*

"In *Marriage and Other Acts of Charity*, Kate Braestrup, a widowed and recently remarried, youngish Unitarian minister, is enthusiastic about the institution of marriage and gives what we can take as a traditional defense, together with personal anecdotes and tasteful biblical citations—the very book to give to a newlywed, Christian-leaning couple: marriage isn't easy but can lead to personal growth." —Diane Johnson, *New York Review of Books*

"This memoir from a twice-hitched minister is the most honest you may ever read about the roller-coaster ride of marriage. Coupled or single, you'll enjoy the ride." —Elisabeth Egan, *Self*

"Fans of Braestrup's richly enlightening *Here If You Need Me* will surely love *Marriage and Other Acts of Charity,* which continues the story of her life as the backdrop for her observations and meditations as a wife, mother, and woman of the cloth. And what a story it is!...As Braestrup navigates the uncharted waters of a later-in-life romance and a new marriage, she is also witness to the heartbreak and turmoil that love brings to the fragile human heart, especially when so many 'happily-ever-afters' end prematurely in divorce. And, as chaplain, she must also comfort those who are suffering the anguish of irrevocable loss—when death takes a loved one. 'Life is short,' she recognizes, 'and pain engraves its memories in your flesh....Love whoever needs what you have; love the ones who have been placed in your path.' In *Marriage and Other Acts of Charity,* with grace and style, Braestrup leads the way." —Linda Stankard, *BookPage*

"Braestrup believes that 'every soul is called to love and serve' and her advice remains straightforward and simple—love more." —*Booklist*

"A talented spinner of tales...Braestrup's sense of humor is spot-on." —Janet Okoben, *Cleveland Plain Dealer*

"The dialogue is deft and elegant, the scenery and back stories interesting and intense. The game wardens of Maine live on an icy edge between life and death; Braestrup evokes that world with skill." —Carolyn See, *Washington Post*

"Listen to Kate Braestrup for any time at all, and her essential kindness reveals itself....Braestrup's voice is intimate and a little smoky, and she's funny and humble, whether she's sharing humorous stories or heartrending ones." —*AudioFile*

MARRIAGE

and

OTHER ACTS

of

CHARITY

KATE BRAESTRUP

A REAGAN ARTHUR BOOK

BACK BAY BOOKS

LITTLE, BROWN AND COMPANY

NEW YORK   BOSTON   LONDON

ALSO BY KATE BRAESTRUP

Onion

Here If You Need Me

Beginner's Grace: Bringing Prayer to Life

Copyright © 2010 by Kate Braestrup
Reading group guide copyright © 2011 by Kate Braestrup and Little, Brown and Company
Excerpt of *Here If You Need Me* copyright © 2007 by Kate Braestrup

Reagan Arthur / Back Bay Books
Little, Brown and Company
Hachette Book Group
237 Park Avenue, New York, NY 10017
www.hachettebookgroup.com

Originally published in hardcover by Reagan Arthur / Little, Brown and Company, January 2010
First Reagan Arthur / Back Bay paperback edition, January 2011

Reagan Arthur Books is an imprint of Little, Brown and Company. The Reagan Arthur Books name and logo are trademarks of Hachette Book Group, Inc.

The publisher is not responsible for websites (or their content) that are not owned by the publisher.

Library of Congress Cataloging-in-Publication Data
Braestrup, Kate.
   Marriage and other acts of charity : a memoir / Kate Braestrup.
      p. cm.
   ISBN 978-0-316-03191-2 (hc) / 978-0-316-03190-5 (pb)
   1. Braestrup, Kate.   2. Authors, American—20th century—
Biography.   3. Clergy—Maine—Biography.   4. Married people—United States—Biography.   I. Title.
   PS3552.R246Z47 2009
   813'.54—dc22
   [B]   2009008492

10   9   8   7   6   5   4   3   2   1

RRD-IN

Printed in the United States of America

To Simon, my husband

Marriage, n: a community consisting of a master, a mistress and two slaves, making in all, two.

—Ambrose Bierce, *The Devil's Dictionary*

MARRIAGE

and

OTHER ACTS

of

CHARITY

CHAPTER ONE

One summer day, my daughters, Ellie and Woolie, ages eight and six, respectively, got lost in the Maine woods. They went for a walk with their older brothers, but Zachary and Peter, tired of their sisters' slower pace, abandoned them in what, from the girls' point of view, was a vast and trackless wilderness.

Actually, it was a small wilderness, situated on an extremely small island off Popham Beach, Maine. The kids and I were staying there for an August weekend.

We had watched ospreys fishing. We pored over tide pools where sea stars slowly bored their lethal holes in the shells of dog whelks, and barnacles waved their thready tentacles in the water, hoping to catch a snack of minute marine debris. Right after breakfast on our first day, the kids spotted a seal's tidy domed head just off the rocky beach and seated themselves in a blond row in the blond grass on the bluff above, waiting for the seal to pop her head up again.

They looked just like a painting by Mary Cassatt, I thought—my aesthetic judgment once more overwhelmed by maternal feeling. Later, when Zach and Peter returned from their walk with the news that they had left their tiresome sisters behind and had no idea what had become of them, what followed was not a scene Mary Cassatt would have wanted to paint. (Edvard Munch might have taken a stab at it.)

Meanwhile, Ellie and Woolie sat glumly beneath a spruce, convinced they would never see home and hearth again. Then it occurred to Ellie that they were, after all, on an island. If they found the shoreline, it should be possible, in theory, to circumambulate the island and find, by the water's edge, the cottage with their mother in it. So the girls struck off in the direction of the nearest wave sounds, and when they reached the coast, they turned right. The plan would have worked perfectly, except that in scrambling over a particularly jagged set of rocks, Ellie fell, cutting her knee badly.

Things now looked very bleak. Ellie bewailed her bloodied knee. Woolie toyed with the idea of building a hut out of driftwood and nursing her sister back to health on a diet of rainwater and raw clams, but Ellie's knee really did look painful. Besides, Woolie could do with a cookie. So Woolie threw back her head and addressed herself to the empty sky.

"HELP!" she shrieked. "HELP! WE'RE LOST, AND MY SISTER IS *BLEEDING!*"

Within moments, a paramedic was by her side.

Maternal panic was replaced that day by bewildered gratitude. Woolie marched jauntily into view, followed by her sister, borne in the arms of a stranger, her injured knee neatly bandaged.

"Glad to help," said the paramedic. His name was Joel. He happened to be vacationing with his family in a cottage on the other side of the island and had been peacefully sunning himself when the summer breeze carried Woolie's cri de coeur to his trained ears.

Woolie seemed to take it as a matter of course that her prayers would be answered. If she had known the word *paramedic*, she might even have been more specific in her request, although, as it turned out, she didn't need to be.

I am a person of faith or a religious fanatic, depending on whom you ask. I believe absolutely in God made manifest in love, but I can't explain, let alone emulate, my daughter's confidence in life's beneficence. When in doubt, I reflexively anticipate the worst.

Pessimism meshes well with my primary ministry, which is to serve as chaplain to the Maine Warden Service. I provide support and comfort to game wardens and civilians at the scenes of the various outdoor calamities to which game wardens respond: snowmobile accidents, freshwater boating accidents and drownings, hunting accidents, suicides, wilderness search and rescue operations, and, occasionally, a homicide.

No one needs a chaplain when the outcome is likely to be good, so quite a lot of my work deals with death. Or to put it differently, and as I prefer to think of it, I bear witness to the ways in which love resurrects itself in the face of loss. It is a great honor to be present to a stranger's grief, to play even a small part in the most intimate, excruciating, and transformative chapter in a person's and family's history. I appreciate the clarity and frankness of those whose loved ones have died. ("Death just strips away all the bullshit," declared a hospital chaplain I know, approvingly.)

Having written at length about death already, I realized that it must be possible to describe how love—real love, God's love—manifests itself in other areas of life, those in which everyone involved continues breathing. Certainly a more cheerful topic.

I've been married and widowed, betrayed and betrothed. Moreover, as a woman of the cloth, I am often called on to advise others about how to enter into, be content within, or extract themselves from the married state. At frequent intervals I preside over the nuptial ceremonies of neighbors, friends, and game wardens. *Write what you know*, they say.

On the other hand, far from encouraging us to strip away what is trivial and false, marriage starts out with the expensive theatrics of a wedding. If national statistics hold for the couples who ask me to join them in holy matrimony, 50 percent of them will end up divorced. The more surprising statistic I offer to the eager affianced is this: 100 percent of marriages will end.

So what was I thinking? Marriage isn't a cheerful subject at all!

I, of all people, should know this: My young late husband, Drew, was killed in a car accident, and friends, my parents, and my sister have been divorced. Many good friends and colleagues are making second and even third attempts at this putatively happy state. Whence their Woolie-ish, senseless confidence? Why are they not rushing to join monasteries and nunneries? This would be the sensible response to the pain that, once endured, convincingly promises more to come. Instead we stand (or stand again) in a place made holy by this reliable human lunacy and offer heartfelt prayers in the direction of a sky that has already demonstrated its indifference to heartbreak. Our mothers and brothers smile, our sisters weep, and little children scatter flower petals at our feet as if what we are doing makes sense, but it makes no sense. It is crazy to marry, nuts to love! It's crazy to risk loving even the mother, the brother, the matron of honor. It's insane to love *at all*. God help us, we do it anyway.

Once upon a time, a man named Paul wrote a letter to a fledgling congregation of Christians at Corinth. He wrote in Koine Greek, and included lines destined to be quoted at millions of Christian wedding ceremonies, concluding with the line that begins "And now faith, hope and love abide."

The word Paul used for *love* was *agape*, later translated into the Latin *caritas*, from which we get our English word *charity*, and so we use the word to describe a certain kind of giving. It is the needy, the unfortunate, the poor and dependent, who require charity, generally in the form of money or material assistance. So when the King James Bible says "the greatest of these is charity," we imagine ourselves virtuously writing checks to the United Way.

Still, *caritas,* like *agape,* is better translated as *love,* but of a wholehearted, impartial, and selfless variety that in its human incarnation is said to hint at the nature of God's love. *Caritas* isn't something only the poor, the sick, or prisoners need, and neither is it necessarily what the rich and healthy are exclusively able to provide. Love takes many forms, from the ludicrously painful profundity of an adolescent crush to the intense, protective passion of a new parent for an infant. There is the lump that rises, unexpectedly, in the throat of an otherwise reliably jaded American on seeing the Statue of Liberty, and there is the presence of a hospice volunteer at the bedside of the dying man. There are sturdy kindnesses and noble heroics, and there are ordinary commitments made and held to, day after day. Marriage is one of these, but there are many others.

In younger days, I scornfully deplored the paucity of synonyms for *love* available to English speakers: "Do you know that there are something like forty-seven words for *love* in Hindi to name the permutations and variations of the thing?" I would rhetorically inquire. But I've grown comfortable with this expressive compression. All loves have much in common, and any one will offer a useful, if not painless, education in the limitations and possibilities of being human. If you give your committed love to a person, an idea, or a cause, even should that person, idea, or cause be taken from you, or proven false, you will be a better lover—of anyone, of anything—for the experience. Because I am as religious person, I see this in characteristically grandiose, religious terms: The point of being human is to get better (and better) at *caritas*, at *agape*, at love.

When asked, I have said that my call to professional ministry was inspired by the startling and to me miraculous abundance of *caritas* made available after my first husband, Drew, died. Friends, neighbors, strangers, took care of us, and with such generosity that I can't think of that painful time in my life without remembering also their absurdly lavish gifts of love. And so it was love, not loss, I was called to honor with my ministry, love that I wished to explore, participate in, and cultivate and through my work.

An expanded answer, however, would have to include the way Drew loved me and I him. This wasn't the same at the end as it was in the beginning. In fact, in a quieter miracle, we did at least begin to learn not only to need, lust after, laugh with, and feel affection for one another, but to offer each other compassion, and a more complete and generous acceptance—in a word, we became more *charitable* toward one another.

This was important and it was difficult. Looking back, I think I withheld my best and most generous love from Drew as if suspicious that he might not reciprocate, or as if reciprocity—a quid pro quo—were necessary. Blindness as to the extent of his generosity toward me was the inevitable corollary. In short, I loved him, but not fearlessly and generously, not with *agape* or anything approaching it. Which is sad, since everyone needs a little *caritas,* sometimes, and almost everyone is, in some way, able to give it. And the funny little secret of love is that the result of the gift is gratitude for both giver and receiver, and therefore joy.

I wish I had learned about this earlier. I am glad I learned it in time.

CHAPTER TWO

I may not be a nun, but I am a woman of the cloth, ordained as a minister and committed to the service of God. If you ask any minister how he or she decided to go into the ministry, the story you get will likely be a love story.

Like in the romantic tales a newlywed will tell, a minister arrives in the pulpit after a journey that seems, in retrospect and in the retelling of the tale, mysterious and blessed. There are encounters that could only have been fated, synchronicities of time and place that had to have been divinely preordained. If the minister is lucky, the story will provide a durable template for understanding subsequent intimations and glimpses of God.

"So what is your story?" A Maine game warden named Jesse Gillespie asked me.

We were lying on our stomachs on a spice-scented bed of leaves in the middle of a forest, a pair of binoculars handy, and Warden Gillespie had just finished educating me about the love life of the North American porcupine. The warden was keeping watch over an illegal deer bait. I don't often participate in the wardens' primary law enforcement responsibility, which is to enforce fish and wildlife law, unless I decide, as I did that day, to tag along.

"Prickly pig" is what the name actually means, he told me, although a porcupine is not a pig but a rodent. And they mate for life. "Now whenever I see a porcupine milling around in the vicinity of a roadkill it just breaks my heart. I need a bumper sticker that says I BRAKE FOR MONOGAMOUS PORCU-PINES." We sighed and were silent for a moment, imagining a porcupine grieving in some dim, bewildered way, beside a road-killed mate.

"How do porcupines mate *at all,* let alone for life?"

You can try posing this to a game warden as a serious question—I did—but you will always get the humorous answer: "Very carefully."

"They have to stay relaxed throughout the encounter to keep the quills—about thirty thousand of them—lying lower than the softer fur that covers their bodies. I'll tell you one thing," said Warden Gillespie. "If porcupines do mate for life, I can see why. Talk about female selectivity! *If she don't want it, it definitely will not happen.* Male porcupines must be really good at sweet talk and foreplay." Warden Gillespie stole a quick glance at my clerical collar and then at my face, as if checking to see whether the word *foreplay* might be too earthy for his chaplain's ears.

"I should think they wouldn't want to abandon a relationship that takes so much trouble to establish," I was saying, and the warden nodded.

"That too," he said.

Some lovely does had turned up, picking through the undergrowth on slender legs. Fastidiously they sniffed, then nibbled the dried bait piled discreetly among the skunk cabbages. Their enormous ears, shaped like lilies, turned and trembled at the slightest sound.

Enraptured, the warden and I watched them from our little redoubt. The deer ate their fill and were off, passing through shafts of sunlight thick with insects before, with a last flick of white tails, they vanished.

Warden Gillespie and I rolled onto our backs and covered our faces with our arms to keep the mosquitoes at bay. I told him the parable of my first marriage, the one that taught me how to serve God.

I can't say I planned to be a minister from the start. Still, it was my childhood ambition to be a really, *really* good person. If I confess this in their presence, my siblings laugh, because I was a famously rotten kid.

"Worse than me?" Peter asks.

I can answer him both truthfully and comfortingly: "Oh, yes, my darling son. Much worse than you."

Still, it wasn't as if I expected to be good right away. My elder sister had the lock on quotidian good behavior, after all; she was mannerly, nonviolent, tidy, and good at school. (Her name is Angelica. Who can compete with *that?*) My brother, meanwhile, didn't have to be good, as far as I could tell. He was a boy.

Moody, volatile, the redundant second girl, I was prone to hitting and tears, shoplifting and self-righteousness, contumacy and neurotic self-reproof. I was opposed on principle to school, but when these principles failed to persuade my mother, I became skilled in the fakery of minor ailments. I lied recreationally.

And yet, stirred by tales of serviceable martyrdom, I imagined future feats of noticeable, heroic, *redeeming* goodness. I would pilot the boats that carried the Danish Jews away from the Nazis to safety in Sweden; I would endure Birmingham jail with Martin Luther King Jr.; I would distribute manna in the refugee camps of Biafra—it was Biafra, in those days, where everyone was starving.

This was back in the late 1960s and early '70s, before the Internet and the 24/7 news cycle, but even then it was hard not to notice that the world was filled with suffering. Even given the abundant energy and time I felt sure I would have as an adult, it became clear that I would have to prioritize among the various potential recipients of my largesse. Should I give food to the hungry, protest against injustice, or rescue refugees? What matters most, food or freedom? Soybeans or chocolate? Whom should I serve? And how?

Someone famously good—Mother Teresa, I think, though I'm not sure—answered the question this way: *Help those whom God has placed in your path.*

I like it! I get a nice image of myself walking down a well-marked path in the sunshine. I come around a corner and—whoops—there she is. Or there he is: *the person God placed in my path*. And I help this person.

It even happens that way in real life now and then. Once, for example, as a college student, I was crossing Dupont Circle in Washington, D.C., and a woman in front of me tripped and whacked her head on the sidewalk. There was blood everywhere, and if you are looking for an obvious sign that someone needs help, it's hard to beat blood.

I applied direct pressure to the wound with one of my nicer scarves and took her to the emergency room in a taxi. The woman was profuse in her thanks and I left the emergency room happily reacquainted with my old ambition to devote the rest of my days to acts of loving kindness. But then—this is true—it happened again! No more than six weeks later, I was exiting a city bus and the woman in front of me fell off the bus step and whacked her head. Blood everywhere: Again, I sacrificed a scarf. Again, I hailed a cab.

Was it God's purpose for me that I should just wander around the nation's capital with a pocketful of cab fare, waiting for people to hurl themselves headfirst to the pavement?

God, being irritatingly God-like, answered by tweaking the message: In the taxi en route to the hospital, that second woman began complaining in a loud voice about all the black people on the bus. She was sure that the black people were somehow responsible for her falling, that the black bus driver had stopped the bus in the wrong place, and the black man behind her had been pushy.

"I was behind you," I said. "You were in my path."

The black guy driving the taxi caught my eye in the rear-view mirror, but he didn't say anything. He didn't charge us for the ride. The bigot was effusively grateful to me, but I went home feeling angry and confused, not virtuous. I was sort of wishing I'd left that lady bleeding on the curb and passed by on the other side.

You know, when Mother Teresa began her career in professional charity, she didn't save lives. Her original mission was to remove people who were close to death from the streets of Calcutta and take them to a more peaceful, quiet, Catholic place to die. She didn't forestall death. She didn't even hand out Tylenol. Maybe it would have been better—that is, of more practical value to more people—if she had devoted herself to, say, setting up a health clinic instead of a hospice, or lobbying the U.N.? But Mother Teresa was not a follower of John Stuart Mill. Her actions were not based in utilitarian moral theory. Mother Teresa was a Catholic nun.

I was a young, middle-class white woman when I accompanied the bigot with the bleeding head to the hospital. The cabdriver was a middle-aged African American man. Why did he and I help the injured woman? Because we could. Why did we help her, specifically? *Because she was there.*

You would have done the same, no doubt. By the principles of our traditions and the inclinations of our human hearts, I believe that every soul is called to love and to serve. If you feel called to Professional Goodness, however, and try to answer the call the way I did, by contemplating the bewildering plethora of needs and possibility, it is easy to be overwhelmed, discouraged, or—sadder still—distracted by such grandiose visions that you fail to see what is right in front of you.

Chapter Three

Once, when we were young, and being together was new and quite exciting, Drew took his reluctant leave of me on a city afternoon. We lived in Washington, D.C., at the time. Drew wasn't a cop yet but a photography student at the Corcoran School of Art.

Because it was ludicrously painful to let him go, if only until the following day, I had tears in my eyes as I watched him lope across a busy avenue. When he reached the curb on the other side, he turned, cupped his hands to his mouth, and shouted above the traffic: "Hey! I love you! Do you love me?" and a homeless man, hobbling slowly up the sidewalk, joined his ancient voice to my response: "Yes! I love you too!" I was twenty.

I was bonkers about Drew and he was bonkers about me. We moved in together and lived in sin in an apartment right across from the National Cathedral. Carefully, Drew selected our first broom at G.C. Murphy on Wisconsin Avenue. We shopped for black beans and rice at the Giant food market. We got a dog.

"What would you think about getting married?" he asked, and I agreed this was a good idea.

Planning the wedding proved tricky. Where would we be married, by whom, and how? There was no family church on either side, no kindly old parson, family rabbi, or well-known parish priest. Not only did we belong to no church, but I for one disapproved strongly of religion. After all, the root word of *religion* means "to bind."

"I'm not into bondage," I informed Drew. "And organized religion has underwritten war, landgrabs, racism, gynophobia, and genocide. Whenever and wherever the human spirit meets organized religion, the delicate rose of true spiritual discernment is inevitably and brutally pruned into soulless doctrine."

What's not to love? Drew said to himself. Or maybe he thought: *Okay, she's a pompous, long-winded know-it-all, but the sex is good.*

Christianity is the organized religion I disapproved of most, naturally enough. It was not Muslim or pagan history I despaired of, not animist or Buddhist self-satisfaction I so wished I could puncture. After all, for all my claims to secularism, my family did celebrate Christmas, not Eid or Passover. The Bible we had on our shelf had not one but two parts, the Old Testament and the New Testament. Christianity was the religion that would bind me if I let down my guard and permitted it to wrap its sticky tentacles around my mortal soul.

"When the revolution comes" (a phrase used in all seriousness by many of my friends), I was sure Christian houses of worship would be torn down or turned into condos with unusually colorful windows. Christian institutions would wither away, Christian leaders would be disgraced or forgotten...

"Other than Martin Luther King Jr., of course," Drew pointed out. "And aren't you the big Tutu groupie?"

"The what?"

Archbishop Desmond Tutu, he explained. "Aren't you a big fan of his?" I had protested apartheid at the South African embassy and had a picture of Tutu in his clerical collar Scotch-taped to our apartment wall.

Stung, I huffed, "You are so immature, so disrespectful, I can hardly be*lieve* it!"

We had a huge fight: tears and accusations, storming around the room enumerating Drew's flaws (me), shouting "Shut UP!" and slamming the door behind him (Drew). Slamming the door was evidence of male violence, an assertion of male privilege: I explained this to Drew later, after we had made up, after we had been passionate, rested in one another's arms, and, thus refreshed, were ready for another fight.

Drew's family came from Tennessee and West Virginia; mine from Park Avenue and Scarsdale. Everyone in my family of origin had been to college; almost no one in his family had. My family were mostly Democrats; most in his family, including Drew himself, were registered Republicans. There were, in short, enough sharp differences between us to make friends and relatives on both sides of the church aisle shake their heads and wonder what on earth would become of our union.

"Marriage is a lot of work," wise friends said.

"*Hard* work," our relatives reiterated. "And you're awfully young."

Well, we *were* young. Our bodies were strong and definitely inclined toward procreation. Perhaps our skeptical relations were right and matrimony was like a West Virginia coal mine. So be it. We would dig.

Naturally, we would write our own ceremony. To do this, as it turned out, we would have to come up with a religion. No problem. I had done it before.

At the age of nine, I had invented a religion. Everyone knows that a religion worth its salt requires scripture, so I wrote a book of scripture on paper dyed sepia with cold coffee, burning the edges of the pages to lend an aura of mystical antiquity. I decided, also for the aesthetics of the thing, that my adherents should wear colorful turbans.

Unfortunately, by the time I was a young adult, I had lost that childhood pentateuch and couldn't remember what my doctrines had been. All I could recall were the turbans, and I doubted my bridesmaids would go for those.

Drew and I would have to start from scratch.

"We could get married in nature," said Drew. "Maybe in Rock Creek Park."

"Maybe," I said doubtfully. It sounded good in theory, but nature, at least in summertime, in Washington, DC, was an awfully humid and buggy venue.

"Where, then?" said Drew.

June was looming. Drew contracted a series of terrible upper-respiratory infections, and I lost ten pounds. Neither of us slept well. Having delivered an accusatory lecture about male hypocrisy and the Madonna-whore complex, I went and bought a white dress and white shoes. We defaulted to plain engraved invitations. We got bogged down in our attempts to write vows that encapsulated our intentions without using loaded traditional words such as "love…honor…cherish…"

After all the effort, all the struggle with feminist texts, the hours spend poring over books of solipsistic poetry and the Bhagvad Gita, Mary Daly and Andrea Dworkin, Khalil Gibran and *For Colored Girls Who Have Considered Suicide/ When the Rainbow Is Enuf,* finally we just ran out of time. In the end, exhausted, we were married in a Catholic chapel (the historic Dahlgren Chapel at Georgetown University). Despite the vestigal taint of the patriarchal transfer of bride as property from one male to another, Dad walked me down the aisle. Presiding over the ceremony was a woman who, however progressive and female she might be, was an ordained Christian minister, the Methodist chaplain of students at Georgetown.

Stranger still, it *worked.* Pale and trembling, Drew and I promised to love and honor each other until we were parted by death. A particularly gruesome crucifix dangled over us, adding grim oomph to the vows. However vague our understanding of the Divine might have been, however confused about what form our joint and joining communion should take, there was no doubt whatever that this was a truly religious ceremony, and binding.

Over the course of our prenuptial meetings, the minister had teased forth from us both an animating idea, a sort of theme for the wedding, which she could then elucidate in her homily. The theme Drew and I offered was a rather starchy one: Our union, we believed, would provide a strong and stable platform from which each of us might sally forth in dedicated service to the community and to the world.

However grandiose this sounds—how much service could Drew and I, two unemployed students of photography and English, respectively, really offer?—this theme too turned out to be a prescient, binding vow.

"And now faith, hope, and love abide," the minister said. "These three; and the greatest of these is love" (First Corinthians 13).

Well, I thought smugly when this was read at our wedding, *one thing we do know how to do is love.*

We were young and passionate, bad tempered, arrogant, affectionate, ignorant. "Do you promise to love and honor for as long as you both shall live?" the minister asked. Drew and I promised, and were bound.

CHAPTER FOUR

Marriage is a three-ring circus," goes an old joke. "The engagement ring, the wedding ring, and suffering."

"You know," I said to Drew eight or nine years later, during one of what had become very frequent discussions of the subject, "our marriage would be fine if you would just resolve your anger issues."

In those nine years, we had moved to Maine. I had written and published a novel. Drew had joined the Maine State Police and meandered along some interesting byways in Maine law enforcement. He served as a road trooper, as an undercover narcotics investigator, a K-9 handler, and a civil rights enforcement officer. Reproducing with the mindless prolificacy of wood lice, we were now the proud parents of four adorable children, and in 1991 we were finally able to buy an ancient house in the friendly old town of Thomaston. Our house boasted a large yard with a garden and enormous trees. Geraniums bloomed with enthusiasm on the sills of our south-facing windows hung with inexpensive lace. The children regarded the alarming hills and valleys in the wide pine-board floors as an amenity designed with toys cars in mind. (That we could not afford furniture also allowed them expansive room for cardboard-box castles.) With the glacial speed our finances permitted, Drew and I were sure we could eventually rehabilitate the place. In the meantime, the kids were happy. They were healthy. We were healthy. But, increasingly, we weren't so happy; at least not with each other. So we signed up for marriage counseling.

I walked into the counselor's office fully prepared to prove the obvious: The marriage was a mess, and it was *not my fault*. At the counselor's gentle prompting, we named some issues. We assigned responsibility. The issues were Drew's. The responsibility was Drew's.

"He has problems with aggression and anger," I said.

"Why don't you talk to Drew," the counselor suggested gently.

"Moreover, I believe he...that is...Drew, I believe *you* feel that, as a woman, I am obliged to put up with your behavior."

"No, I..." Drew began.

"I have made a thorough and I think I can say *dispassionate* examination of our marriage, its structures, its sexual politics, and its relationship to the social order...It is clear to me that the problem in our marriage is—not to put too fine a point on it—*you*."

I read a lot of feminist theory in those days. Drew had

read feminist theory too. In fact, when Drew was a candidate for the Maine State Police, he underwent the usual polygraph test, and one of the standard, if disquieting, questions asked of him was whether he had ever committed rape. Citing the feminist Andrea Dworkin, Drew launched into an explanation about how in jurisdictions lacking a criminal statute specifically outlawing marital rape, wives do not have the legal right to say no to their husband's advances. "If a woman doesn't have the right to say no," Drew told the startled polygraph examiner, "her 'yes' is meaningless. Given that my wife and I currently reside in the District of Columbia, where no law prohibits marital rape, you could say that I have raped my wife repeatedly." (The examiner gave this considerable thought before formulating his next question, which he asked, at last, with care: "*Other* than your wife, Mr. Griffith, have you raped anyone?") Still, Drew's familiarity with the *hermeneutics of radical suspicion* did him no good in marriage counseling.

"I know I'm hard to live with," he said glumly.

"Do you still have sexual relations?" the counselor asked, and we looked at him as if he were crazy. *Of course* we still had sexual relations!

"That's good." The counselor smiled.

"Do you know anything about Zen Buddhism?" he went on. "Well, in Zen Buddhism, a koan is a little word puzzle given by a master to the disciple to solve. *What is the sound of one hand clapping?* That sort of thing. The idea is that working the koan will bring the disciple further along the road to enlightenment." He beamed at us.

"Yes?" Drew said when the counselor didn't continue.

"Your marriage is a living, breathing koan. You have said that you love each other, you still are physically attracted to each other, you have four children whom you are both devoted, to, and nine years ago you made binding vows to one another."

"Yes, but..."

"There are many important reasons to work for the success of this relationship. Given your...er...interests, Kate, you might find it helpful to regard your marriage as a spiritual state...really, a spiritual discipline."

"Well, of course," I said, shooting a pointed look in the direction of my husband. "*I* have no problem with that," I said.

"Ah," said the counselor noncommitally.

If our marriage was a koan, it was the one that Ambrose Bierce articulated nicely in his *Devil's Dictionary:* Marriage is "a community consisting of a master, a mistress and two slaves, making in all, two."

A marriage does create a very small, cloistered community, marked as a convent or monastery is marked, by shared living space, shared resources, and, of course, specific restrictions on sexual behavior. A monastery is characterized not only by the shared spiritual values of its communicants but also by the discipline under which they agree to live. *The Rule of St. Benedict,* for instance, arranged the lives of monks and nuns in cloisters all over Europe, and continues to do so down to the present day. Benedict emphasized obedience, patience, moderation in speech, the sharing of possessions, and the need to be content with menial tasks. "We are therefore to establish a school of the Lord's service in which we hope to introduce nothing harsh or burdensome," Benedict declares in the prologue to his *Rule.* Bad-tempered monks and nuns wouldn't last long in a Benedictine order... or maybe a Benedictine order wouldn't have lasted long if the *Rule* permitted tantrums.

Along with his dry skin and cement-block-shaped head, I inherited my father's temper. There is temper on Drew's side of the family as well, so both of us had the genes for angry behavior, and perhaps enough enculturation so that it seemed normal.

The anger in our marriage claimed casualties: Pencils were snapped, doors slammed, innumerable cups and mugs smacked with irritated emphasis against hard surfaces. Car doors were slammed and kicked, and the car itself was driven out of the driveway with an expressive scream of tortured tires.

Drew put his foot through the screen door once. Knocking imperiously for his attention, I cracked a window. Oh, and then there was that sweet little coffee table, made of cherry. It was the only nice piece of furniture we owned, yet in response to some insufferable spousal insult, I lifted, hurled, and smashed it.

He that is slow to anger is better than the mighty: Yea, and he keepeth his furnishings intact too. Well, we hadn't read Proverbs at the time, or Thich Nhat Hanh, or *The Dance of Anger.* You would think the pathetic sight of the coffee table standing staggered on its broken cherry legs would by itself have brought us both to our senses. Still, if anger was always and everywhere evil, the way would have been clear, wouldn't it? Even to people like us. But anger isn't always a bad thing.

Not in the Bible at least: God, to name one splenetic Being, conveys His divine ire at injustice and immorality through the rantings of his prophets. The prophet Elishah goes so far as to conjure she-bears to maul small boys in response to taunts that, frankly, seem rather mild from my perspective. ("Go away, baldhead!" is the childish slur that sealed their doom.) Though the scripture does not describe Jesus as a chronically choleric man, it is difficult to imagine the moneylenders and dove sellers being cleared from the Temple in Jerusalem by his mildly observing (rather than shouting) that the place had become "a den of thieves." And then, on his way home from cleansing the temple, Jesus has a really weird moment.

The story is repeated in Matthew and Mark (though skipped by Luke and John). Jesus is hungry, we are told, "and seeing a fig tree by the side of the road, he went to it, and found nothing at all on it but leaves." (Mark's Gospel adds a matter-of-fact arboricultural explanation for this deficiency:

"It was not the season for figs.") "Jesus said to the fig tree 'May no fruit ever come from you again!' And the fig tree withered at once" (Matthew 21:18–19; Mark 11:12–14).

My father did odd things like this when his blood sugar was low. His wife, friends, and children became skilled at proffering explanations and apologies to strangers in the vicinity. ("Sorry about your fig tree... do you by any chance have a breadstick?") Of course, we are not meant to see the cursing of the fig tree as a sign that Jesus was hypoglycemic. The disciples were more interested in *how* Jesus had wrecked the tree than in *why* he would do so. Jesus says that if they have sufficient faith in their hearts, they too will be able to wither fig trees, or even chuck mountains into the sea, which, again, sounds less like a miracle and more like the sort of asinine thing Drew and I used to do in the midst of a marital dispute. Maybe this is why Jesus' explanation (such as it is) of why he zapped an inoffensive tree concludes with reassurance about God's forgiveness. If you lose your temper and do something idiotic and destructive, God will understand—He's been there.

"Virtue is not always amiable." John Adams admitted this to himself in his own diary, when the depredations of the Crown had spurred him and his colleagues to a fury that in the end proved the creation of a country. When the gentle Gentile Danish citizens rescued their Jewish compatriots from the Nazis, their heroism was given a jump start by the anger that the German occupation had provoked in them. Anger too pressed America's African Americans and other justice-seekers to ignore their fears of violence or failure and press their righteous cause. And it is in anger that abused spouses often find the courage to leave their partners and find new and safer lives. "Anger is one of the sinews of the soul," said Milton, and to renounce it completely is to maim oneself.

Driving to Washington, DC, to visit my sister, I decided to cut the twelve-hour drive in half and find a motel for the night.

"With a pool," the children chorused, and I, a young new widow inclined to indulge my little ones, agreed. In Connecticut, we found a motel with the requisite amenity, and within a half hour of check-in, the children were happily splashing around in the shallow end.

To my relief, there were no other guests who might be annoyed or inconvenienced by the presence of four small, shrieking swimmers. So I settled myself on a chaise near the edge of the pool and opened a book.

The indoor pool was surrounded on two sides by enormous plate-glass windows that looked out onto a monotonous motel garden. A jogger went by on a concrete path and paused to look in at us; *Poor guy,* I thought fleetingly. *He'd probably planned a nice quiet swim…*

I went back to my book. A few minutes later the jogger appeared, now clad in bathing trunks and apparently undaunted by the noise and tumult in the water.

Sliding into the pool at the deep end, he smiled ingratiatingly at me and I smiled briefly back. He swam a few desultory laps, as solitary adult swimmers generally do, then turned and did a leisurely breaststroke in the direction of my children.

I looked up.

"Hello," he said to the kids.

"Hello," Zach answered politely, and Peter echoed him. The girls paddled over near the pool steps but otherwise ignored the jogger. They were still little enough to get away with being too shy for manners.

"Do you like swimming?" The man swam nearer. "I love to play in the water..." He splashed with his hands. "Isn't this fun?"

"Yes, sir," said Zach. Peter had edged over so he was treading water behind his older brother.

Now, maybe this guy was just lonesome, a father on a business trip who missed his own kids. Maybe. But my book was in my lap; my head was up. My eyes fixed on him, unblinking.

"Come here, little fella," he was saying to Zach, holding out his hands. "You look like a good swimmer. I'll throw you up in the air and you can splash down..."

The man had maneuvered himself so that he was between us, and Zach had to look past his shoulder to shoot me an anxious glance. "No thank you, sir," he replied.

"Come on," the man was saying, holding out his hands, almost touching Zach's chest. "It'll be fun."

I was at the edge of the pool. I don't remember moving to

that place, but I can still vividly feel the concrete edge gripped tightly with my curled toes.

"*He said no,*" I said. At least that's what I think I said. There was a roaring in my ears, and the borders of my vision had contracted into a tight circle around the man's face. "*And you need to get out of the pool right now.*"

Did I say that? I must have said something, but whatever I said, and whatever my tone, the man did remove himself from the water very quickly, and scuttled through the lobby door with his towel clutched to his stomach, never to be seen again.

Okay, so maybe he was just a regular nice man with a few boundary issues.

Maybe.

"I didn't like that guy," Peter remarked.

"Neither did I," I said.

I had been ready to kill him. I don't mean this metaphorically. If that man had not removed his body from between my children and me, if he had not departed the pool and its environs, there would have been blood in the water. I can still feel the hair on the nape of my neck rise and the adrenaline surge into my arms and legs, even into my teeth, when I think of him. *Don't mess with my babies.*

If we assume I had not behaved like a paranoid lunatic, but rather accurately ascertained a threat to my children, this was a moment when anger proved useful. But every difficulty, challenge, or cross word is not a threat and need not be countered with the emotional equivalent of a ballistic missile. Drew and I had begun lobbing missiles at each other every time we had a disagreement, which is to say every day.

Were we incompatible or mentally ill, or had we just developed a very bad habit? If the latter, it was one that certain strains in American culture tend to encourage. We were both familiar with the notion, for example, that suppressing anger was harmful and expressing it through some display of aggression was supposed to serve as a healthy catharsis. "It's bottled-up emotion that causes men to have so many heart attacks and strokes," Drew would say. "I need to get it out."

I, meanwhile, claimed my own anger was linked to the cause of female equality, necessary to the struggle to seek my own personhood rather than yield to an entrenched, unjust patriarchy.

There was some truth in this, of course, just as there is doubtless some truth in the notion that an expression of anger can sometimes clear the air, relieve the nerves, or provoke the conversation one might otherwise too easily avoid. Still, in retrospect it's hard to see how Drew had earned my putatively feminist scorn. He did half the housework. He spent virtually all of his nonworking hours with his children, while his working hours, however interesting and "fulfilling" the job was, could be both exhausting and hazardous.

During that decade of our marriage, four of Maine's police officers were killed in the line of duty. The trooper

David Veillieux was killed in a car accident; the Lewiston police officer David Payne was ambushed and murdered by a drug dealer, the trooper Giles Landry was shot dead by the husband of a battered wife, and the trooper Jeff Parola died in a car accident.

Drew knew these men. He went to their funerals. To muffled drums, in the company of grieving colleagues, he marched in silence through the streets of a Maine hometown. He saluted the bier, stood at attention for "Taps," saw the widows and orphans flinch at the first report of the twenty-one-gun salute. I wrote condolence letters to the families, and our children sent handmade cards.

I wonder if Drew and I used anger as a way of dulling our perception of the fearsome obvious: that sometimes cops go to work and do not come home. Anger is a common anesthetic in law enforcement marriages. The side effects are tough, though, and you tend to need more and more of this drug to get the same effect.

Let's imagine that Drew came home from work late. His lateness meant that I didn't get to the library before it closed. In response, I shrieked obscenities.

What could I do the next time I was provoked to an equivalent degree? Or let's say the insult, on the next occasion, was actually worse? Let's say I didn't get to go to the library, *and* he forgot to pick up the Sunday *New York Times*?

The threshold for the expression of mere annoyance had been set at Shrieked Obscenities. If I merely shrieked obscenities at this more hideous transgression, the adrenaline kick would not be as strong and the anesthetic effect less pronounced, and besides, a crucial nuance in meaning would fail to be communicated. So this time, I should shriek obscenities and smash a coffee table. (*Ahhhhhh.*)

Naturally, Drew and I were, at the same time, parents trying to set and hold appropriate boundaries. The children weren't allowed to shriek obscenities, or strike each other, or break things. If they did any of these, they were disciplined, even spanked, though this was rare. Rarity is what I remember, anyway. Peter offers a different estimate as to the frequency of corporal punishment. His behind, he claims, would bear more than a few handprints were it not for the forgiving resilience of adipose tissue.

This is probably obvious, but I will declare it anyway: I thought the guy in the motel pool was a child molester. I was afraid he was going to injure, frighten, or traumatize my children. What the hell were Drew and I afraid of that made the adrenaline surge through our limbs and into our jaws, our teeth bared and prepared for biting? That's what the therapist wanted to know.

"What are the issues?" he asked.

Did I say something like "I am afraid that Drew will die or be badly hurt at work and it is easier to be angry than afraid"?

Did Drew say "I am wearied, drained dry by what I encounter in my work. I want to be comforted"?

No.

Instead: "These are the issues," I said, and named them one by one.

1. Drew's temper and his tantrums were the outward manifestation of an underlying and apparently incurable character disorder.
2. My tantrums were justifiable expressions of the stresses of stay-at-home motherhood and the various deprivations thereof.
3. These various deprivations were not par for the course for a mother of four but were unique, and were his fault.
4. That my emotional state had nothing whatsoever to do with the time of the month, and if he were to suggest such a thing, it was evidence of what an ignorant, insensitive bastard he really, truly was, and no, I'm not going to keep my voice down—I have the right to express my feelings... etc., etc.
5. He yelled too much and too loudly and scared the children.
6. That these and other parenting mistakes were not adequately countered by his steadfast affection for them.
7. As their mother, and a person who had done considerable research into the proper way to parent, I was the sole judge of what was and was not a parenting mistake.
8. When the children turned out bad it would be his fault.

9. Because he was larger, louder, and male, his temper was intrinsically more threatening and problematic than mine.
10. Everything in our marriage—indeed, everything in my life—would be just fine if Drew just got his goddamned act together.
11. Everything in my life might be fine if I just didn't have to deal with Drew at all.

It was a familiar and convincing list. At least Drew was convinced. By now he believed me when I said that living with him was horrible and living without him would be an improvement. He was even willing to believe, up to a point, anyway, that our problems were really his problems. So Drew began to work the koan: He went for individual counseling. He joined a men's group and talked about male anger and its sources, and possible cures. (Item number 12: Drew selfishly goes to men's group instead of spending time with me and the children.) These measures began to work. They generally do, which is why they are so often recommended. Drew was a very disciplined person, and—bless his noble heart—he did actually want to stay married. To me.

Meanwhile, I talked about divorce. We were out in the backyard with the kids. Peter was on the swing, begging his father to give him pushes. I told Drew why I wanted to break up (see items 1–12, above). He listened.

"I never thought I would lose you," Drew said at last,

sadly and with heartbreaking dignity, but I was too angry to hear him.

Anger pushes us past limitations imposed by physical weakness, cowardice, or conscience. To make a habit of anger, however, is to make a habit of bashing through the boundaries, one after another, until you get to the last wall.

"I want a divorce," I said to Drew in the backyard of our house as Peter called across the lawn.

"Dada! Push me!"

"I'm serious," I said. Was I?

Was this just more melodrama, another escalation in the Look How Pissed I Am This Time arms race toward marital Armageddon? I can't remember. Like the feel of my palm striking Peter's little bum, it's been stricken from my memory.

CHAPTER FIVE

So I was sitting on the beach with my husband," said my friend Monica, "and out of the corner of my eye, I saw him passionately kiss the babysitter."

"Oh my God," I said.

"I almost vomited," she continued calmly, "though of course, I was hallucinating. He wasn't anywhere near the babysitter. But the pain was terrible nonetheless." Monica was telling this story to comfort me. I was in need of comfort. I was freaking out.

We were in my kitchen, having coffee. Both of us were liberally anointed with grease and birdseed. I had just led the children—her three, my four—through one of what Monica refers to as "Kate's Lunatic Craft Activities." Melted lard, mixed with birdseed, is pressed into empty frozen juice containers to mold bird feeders that can be hung on backyard trees. It had been one of the activities memorable more for lunacy than craft: The children mashed the mess around for a while, tasted it, threw it at one another, then lost interest and toddled off to play Ninja Turtles. (Months later, Drew and I would still be prying seeds out of the action figures' greasy little joints.)

The previous day's mail had delivered a huge shock. Drew received a postcard from a female friend of his, and when I saw a woman's name signed with affection and didn't immediately recognize it, I came close to fainting.

"It was so strange," I told Monica. "I mean, for once I wasn't pissed off. My first thought wasn't *That bastard is going to have some splainin' to do when he gets home!* It was as if he were never coming home. Like he was gone, forever—POOF, BAM—just like that."

"It's an awful feeling," Monica commiserated.

"Sick," I said. "Right here." I pointed at my stomach just below my sternum.

"Exactly," Monica agreed.

What I didn't tell Monica was that the second thought I had, after the first (which wasn't so much a thought as a cluster of physical sensations: hands so suddenly weak the mail fell out of them, lungs abruptly deprived of air, and knees bereft of the strength to stand), was this: *And why, exactly, would he want to stay?*

"Don't be an idiot," Drew had said when I told him about the postcard. "I love you." He was home, still in uniform. He hugged me against his Kevlar-stiffened chest. "I'm not going anywhere. I'm right here."

"Okay," I said, wrapping my arms around his waist above

the unyielding line of his gun belt, pressing my cheek against the cold metal edges of his badge. "Okay."

Don't be an idiot, but I was one.

A revelation reveals the mismatch between what you had always thought of as truth (if you had bothered to think about it at all) and a better, *truer* truth. The scientist, the artist, the composer, the lover, the poet, and the cop all experience revelations large and small.

In fact, "revelation" is probably marked more by the sensory experience than by the specific content or context of what is revealed. Unlocking a heretofore intractable scientific question probably prompts the same physical sensations (shortness of breath, tinnitus, emotional lability) in the scientist that the poet feels when she is sure, at long last, that the perfect stanza is gliding free from her pen. "Surprised by joy," the theologian C. S. Lewis called it, and a cop who is finally snapping the handcuffs around the wrists of a dangerous and elusive perpetrator might know exactly what Lewis meant.

Such moments can present themselves so powerfully that the earth seems to shudder and the clouds to sing. Yanked up and plunked down, you find your feet have been set upon a new path.

Well, that's one metaphor. Others could be used. In fact, some might be offended by the comparison, but when the ordinary comfort of my husband's embrace resolved what must be admitted to be a pathetically common little emotional crisis, I finally got a glimpse of what a Christian might mean when she talks about being born again.

"I don't know how to love him…what to do, how to mo-o-ove him…" I sang dolefully—then interrupted myself: "Knock it off, Peter Rabbit!"

Two days or so after the Day of the Postcard, I was, as usual, driving somewhere in a car filled with small children. Peter was kicking the back of my seat. I could see him in my rearview mirror, his beautiful little rosebud mouth turned downward in a scowl, his plump little arms crossed defiantly over the chest strap of his seatbelt. He was still smarting from that morning's scolding. Ellie had discovered that the plastic frozen pop maker in the freezer was filled with urine. Peter was not upset at being punished, but he deeply resented having been so quickly identified as the prime—indeed, the *only*—suspect in the case.

"It might not have been me. I'm not *always* the bad boy."

"Peter, I mean it…"

"I…don' know how to…y-u-u-u-v 'im," warbled Woolie.

I mean, if Drew actually asked for something, that would be one thing. But if he doesn't ask…what happens then? Do I just make it up?

I know! I thought. *I could always think about what I might want in a given situation and use that as a rough guide.* And then I thought: *Wow…I'd better write that down!*

When the kids and I got home, Drew would be waiting for us. Peter would confess the crime du jour. "Ellie ate a pissicle," he would explain solemnly. Drew would laugh, of course. Peter's little face would shine with incredulous relief, with delight.

I would tell Drew about the first achievement of my new spiritual journey: I had proudly reinvented the Golden Rule.

In the Bible, the experience of revelation tends to be painful and terrifying. Not surprisingly, perhaps, those who receive revelations are generally not depicted as actively seeking them. Saul of Tarsus was on his way to Damascus, a trip he had presumably made many times in his enthusiasm for persecuting Christians, when suddenly he was flung to the ground. It is described as a kind of seizure, complete with optical disturbances and auditory hallucinations, and Saul could have taken himself off to whatever the first century offered in the way of a neuropthalmologist. Instead, he heard the voice of God, and was henceforth Paul (and persecuted).

The Virgin Mary was at home—reading, tradition has it, but in any case not actively seeking divine communion—when the Angel Gabriel appeared with his unsettling news. After an attempt at resistance—"How can this be?" she asked, as if she weren't already miraculously conversing with an angel—Mary laid down her book and bravely (if you think about it) yielded. "Here am I," she said. "Let it be with me according to your word." What follows is a wondrous maternity and an admirable life, but not, frankly, an enviable one.

According to Buddhist hagiography, the young prince Siddhartha too was going along as usual, taking his pampered existence for granted, when in a single day all of the sufferings inherent in human life broke into his reality and compelled his transformation. Siddhartha's life as the original Enlightened One, the Buddha, was blessed and a blessing to many, but you couldn't really call it easy.

These stories proved some consolation when, cringing beneath the merciless gaze of my own eyes, I realized how utterly I had failed to do something simple. I had refused to love the one I loved, the one I had vowed before God to love, the one God had placed not only in my path but in my own damned bed! Remedial Goodness was clearly in order. I would be good *to Drew*.

Simple. "But not easy," as Ronald Reagan would say (although I think he was talking about arming the Contras). It was October, the season of the Jewish high holy days, Yom Kippur, the days of awe, the days of repentance. I went to church, sat beside Drew in our regular pew, and repented, weeping wetly and gratefully into my penitential sleeve (I always forgot tissues) while familiar voices all around me joined in ragged harmony:

Though I may speak with bravest fire…
But have not love…

I looked back at our shared conflicted past through a lens scraped suddenly clean. My marriage had announced its fragility and its inestimable worth in a single afternoon. What had given that experience such impact? Was I overdue for a snack? Premenstrual? Maybe something had been going along under the surface of things for months—years, even—and it only felt like a sudden revelation?

"Or maybe it was the Holy Spirit?" my friend Moira, a fellow student at the seminary, would later offer on hearing the story.

"Is the Holy Spirit always so excruciating?" I asked.

"Um...yes," said Moira, and managed not to add, "Duh."

"I love Drew," I explained to Tonya at the time, in one of our long, anodyne discussions of the subject.

"Of course you do. He loves you too. But it is hard to love a human being. And state troopers are particularly hard to love." (Tonya is married to one, after all.)

Ah, yes. Renouncing anger meant giving up anger's analgesic effects. Now I had to deal head-on with my fears for Drew's safety, my terror of loss.

"That's not what I mean," snapped Tonya briskly. "State troopers are hard to love because they're all paranoid control freaks."

Well, yes. That too.

Whenever Drew came home from work, the first thing he would do was prowl around the house, making sure everything was Under Control.

Now, occasionally everything wasn't *quite* under control. I can admit this: Sometimes I might have left a door unlocked. Big deal. Or maybe I left the teakettle on the hot burner, or a bathtub overflowing or something. It's not like it happened every night…And yet every night, night after night, Drew would go around checking the stove top for smelting pots and the ceilings for suspicious water stains. He would make sure the doors were locked against intruders.

One night I awakened to hear Drew bellowing up the stairs. "Kate? *Kate…KAY-Ate!*"

"Wha…?"

"I need help," he said gloomily. "It's the fish tank."

I looked at my watch. It was three o'clock in the morning. "What *about* the fish tank?"

"It smells of Murphy's Oil Soap."

"Of…?"

"One of the kids must have put Murphy's Oil Soap in the fish tank. Come down. We have to save the fish."

Now. These were not designer fish. They occupied a palatial thirty-gallon tank, with a bubbler and a pink ceramic castle, but they were goldfish, the kind sold at pet shops to people who plan to feed them to their piranhas. The total retail value of our fish was something like $1.27. *And it was three o'clock in the morning.*

"Hurry," Drew hollered. "We have to save the fish!"

The best predictor of future behavior is past behavior, right? If our complicated marital history was anything to go by, the rest of the conversation should have gone like this:

"I'm tired. Come to bed. The fish will be fine."

"The fish will die!"

"Let them die. We'll buy more tomorrow."

"Oh, great. That's just great! What kind of lesson in pet ownership would that be for the kids, huh? What kind of lesson in planetary stewardship would it be?"

"Oh, please. Puh-leeeze. Who are you now, Trooper Tree-Hugger? Don't talk to *me* about planetary stewardship..." And we'd be off, shouting and screeching and slamming things around. Drew would sleep on the couch. We would both be silent and angry for days...

That was how the conversation should have gone, because we were difficult, complicated human beings with baggage and bad tempers, and one of us was a state trooper. So why didn't it go that way?

Because this happened *after*. After the counseling, and the postcard, after the Days of Awe and after Drew and I had, in the sight of God and of our beloved witnesses (all four of them), humbly and with all appropriate awe, declared ourselves irrevocably still married.

I love him, I said to myself. *Nothing matters more than this.*

I got up out of bed and went downstairs. I helped Drew drain all thirty gallons from the fish tank, one gallon milk jug at a time. We rinsed the tank. We rinsed the rocks and the pink ceramic castle. We rinsed the fish. We put thirty gallons of clean water back into the tank, one gallon milk jug at a time. My husband kept gazing at me, his eyes full of wonder: *What have the space aliens done with my real wife?*

We put the fish back into the tank. They swam around. They looked as contented as fish ever look, as grateful as fish ever are. And Drew? Drew was so happy.

It took an hour and a half to do the whole job. Dawn was beginning to glow on the eastern horizon by the time we were done. Was Drew's happiness worth an hour and a half out of my life?

You want the simplest, truest answer?

Yes.

Chapter Six

Here is the sort of insight I just can't resist sharing: "I've solved the toilet seat up/down conundrum!" I told Warden Gillespie excitedly.

"Hallelujah," he said suspiciously.

"I'm thinking of sending 'round an all-wardens memo," I said. "What do you think?"

Here's the solution: Before flushing, all adults and children in a household should be taught to *close the lid of the toilet*. Why? Because when a toilet is flushed, tiny water droplets are flung into the air, bearing with them foul bacteria from sources it would be indecorous to describe, especially while eating lunch, which is (of course) what Warden Gillespie and I were doing when I brought up the subject. "These water droplets float around the room until they land on whatever surface presents itself. Like, say, your toothbrush."

Closing the lid helps keep the bacteria where they belong,

and has the added virtue of not privileging one gender over another. After all, everyone (not just males, not just females) will have the onerous additional task of *lifting something* before piddling, and everyone will have to *put something down* before she or he may consider her or his sojourn in the loo complete.

"Okay, but it seems to me that males will still have to lift *more*," Warden Gillespie pointed out. "I mean, we have to lift the seat and the lid, while females only have to lift the lid."

"That's why men have all that impressive upper-body strength," I told him. "Don't nitpick. I've given you the formula for peace, harmony, and an *E. coli*–free toothbrush."

"Thanks," said Warden Gillespie into his hamburger.

It took time and patience, like nursing a convalescent slowly back to health, but Drew's and my relationship recovered quickly enough that Zach, who was a little boy at the time, remembers it as an overnight transformation.

"You and Dad fought," Zach said to me. "Every day."

He had waited for a year after his father's funeral before allowing himself to speak of the harder parts of the family life that had been lost. He was nine when Drew died, old enough to retain clear memories of daily rhythms and interactions as well as special events. Zach's memories were strong enough to maintain themselves in the face of all of the inevitable memorializing. "It was scary," he remembered.

"I'm sorry, Zackie."

"And then, one day, you just stopped. You stopped, and you never did it again. That's what happened." He looked at me with his large, clear eyes, daring me to contradict him, but his memory, as usual, was accurate.

"Yes, honey-bunny," I said. "That's what happened."

"None of it was what Sergeant Cook would call rocket surgery," I said to Jesse Gillespie, of what happened between Drew and me. "It was all embarrassingly obvious."

We were back at the deer bait. Jesse lay on his stomach, propped on his elbows. He had the binoculars screwed into his eye sockets as he surveyed the area. The sunlight was growing milky, and the air was dense with mosquitoes. Idly, I wondered how may grams of protein I would derive, over time, from the bugs I've breathed in and swallowed.

"So why is it so rare?" he asked reasonably. "That kind of love, I mean?"

Maybe it isn't so rare. I look around myself—at church, for instance—and I see plenty of happily partnered people; Larry and Jean, Rolfe and Susan, Lucy and Annie…Each couple is apparently receiving the sort of honoring and cherishing they bargained for, loving each other for better or worse, for richer, for poorer, in sickness and in health, without a lot of fuss, without making a big drama out of the thing.

Of course, unions are ending too, bangs and whimpers all around. Some result from the inexcusable cruelty of an abusive spouse or from the alcoholic's self-destroying intoxication. Leaving these aside, though, could any garden-variety marriage that is experiencing more common marital problems (boredom, uneven rates of personal growth, an isolated incident of infidelity) theoretically "be saved"?

Tom and Tonya Ballard have a good marriage.

Tonya was a young English teacher making a good salary. She was married to Tom, a newly minted Maine state trooper. Both sensible, conscientious people, they waited to have a child ("What a concept!" as Drew would say) until their work lives were well established and secure. Tonya was so well organized, she had scheduled her pregnancy so the birth would take place in the spring. That way, her six weeks of maternity leave would mesh seamlessly into the summer break, giving her plenty of time to breastfeed and establish her relationship with the baby before putting him or her in daycare and returning to the classroom in the fall.

Two months before he was expected, Michael was born. He weighed barely two pounds. Weeks of nip-and-tuck survival were spent in the hospital before the neonatologist finally removed all the lines and tubes that had kept Michael's tiny body going and declared him fit to go home.

Even then, Michael had to be fed every two hours around the clock. Michael wasn't all that interested in eating. The feedings were prolonged struggles, exhausting for everyone concerned. By the time I met Michael, he had been out of the womb for nine months, but he was still considerably smaller than his new two-month-old buddy Zach. And while Zach would happily consume all the milk I could offer and still had room to try a taste of rice cereal here and there, Michael still had to be coaxed, cajoled, or tricked into eating.

"Putting him in daycare was out of the question," Tonya says. "You couldn't pay someone enough to work as hard as Tom and I had to work just to keep Michael alive."

So Tonya and Tom pared down and lived on what Tom made as a state trooper. Tonya, like me, became a full-time mother.

Tom and Tonya's marriage was and remains a relationship of sexual and reproductive exclusivity, companionship, and affection. Theirs is a relationship undergirded by old rules and venerable social conventions, one that confers practical strength and well-being. Tom and Tonya had to work together to keep Michael breathing, and to keep their family going. These days, they both work (Tonya finally did go back to teaching), and they are now paying for Michael's college education and for that of his little sister, Meghan. Together they have planned for retirement. Each provides encouragement and resources for the other to pursue his or her individual ambitions, and each provides both emotional and financial security in case of disaster. What if the school where Tonya now teaches decides it has to downsize? What if Tom decides he wants to go to graduate school after he retires from the state police? What if, God forbid, a loved one again requires the kind of prolonged, intensive, loving attention that money just can't buy?

* * *

This is what a good marriage can do: This is the kind of security it can provide. For millions, over the millennia, the practical argument for marriage was more than sufficient. Even now, it can seem pretty compelling. So, must everyone experience a religious revelation in and about their marriage?

I made myself very tiresome for a while, proselytizing piously to my long-suffering friends about the inchoate spiritual potential of married love. But if revelation by definition reveals a gap between what is and what could or should be, then any Joe Schmo who is already loving his wife or husband... well, *he's loving his wife or husband*. Maybe his resistance to love will reveal itself elsewhere: in his relationship with his parents or his siblings, his kids, or the Poor and Downtrodden. Maybe he has no resistance to love at all, is gap-free, in which case this particular Joe Schmo walks on water and his friends call him Jesus.

The notion that marriage is an institution peculiarly equipped to promote spiritual growth is an agreeable one for ministers who, after all, perform weddings. In so doing, Christian ministers at least sonorously declare the matrimonial significance of Christ's first miracle. Jesus was at a wedding in Cana when he changed water into wine, and this is taken to mean that he approves of weddings, even though he doesn't actually say so, and never married himself, and besides, it's clear enough from the text that the water-into-wine miracle was his mom's idea, not his. But you'll hear about Cana at just about every Christian wedding you go to, because, truth be told, a Christian pastor really doesn't have a lot of other wedding-related Bible verses to choose from. First Corinthians ("Tho I may speak in tongues of mortals and of angels...") is proffered, but even this is a bit of a stretch, since Paul wasn't referring to married love in this passage. Paul never married either, and his grudging "it is better to marry than to burn [with lust]" is hardly a ringing endorsement of matrimony.

In fact, to the extent that the various books of the Bible mention marriage at all, they seem to take it for granted as a desirable if not, strictly speaking, essential prelude to the procreation of God's people. Otherwise, no particular life-style appears more suited to God's purposes than any other. The patriarchs and prophets of the Hebrew Scripture and the followers and apostles of Jesus in the New Testament are depicted living a variety of ordinary lives, some married with children, others not, when they receive their divine instructions. Moses is hiking along a mountain trail with his sheep, Paul is on a road trip to Damascus, Sarah is cooking supper in her tent, and Samuel is still a child, sound asleep in his bed, when God calls.

"Here I am!" Samuel answers drowsily.

The Virgin Mary is at home, reading, when it is her turn. "Here am I," she says.

Maybe the point isn't to know precisely where or how to find God. Maybe you just need to know how to answer when God at last finds you?

Chapter Seven

Oh, there you are," said Drew. I was ascending the staircase with a pile of clean laundry clasped to my bosom. "I'm going to work. Love you." His uniform was pressed, sharp, his boots and belt and holster gleamed, his Smoky Bear hat was in his hand.

"Can you pick up the *New York Times* on the way home?"

"Sure. I'll try to remember."

I tossed the laundry to the top landing and sat down on the stairs so as to bring my face close enough for kissing. He kissed me. I kissed him.

"We need more milk," he said. "I'll get that too."

"Okay," I kissed him again. He kissed me.

"I'd better go. Good-bye," he said. And stayed, bowing his body so he could lay his head on my lap. I ran my hand over his crew cut. Later, my palm would hold the scent of his hair.

Spring sunlight poured in through the front windows, striping the slanted pine floor boards and dappling the geraniums blooming ruby, rose, and cherry red. "I don't want to go." Drew's voice was full of wonder.

Drew also worked on Sunday the fourteenth of April, 1996. I went to church and sat in our usual pew by myself. My friend Susan sat down beside me, opening her purse with a conspiratorial flourish. "Have you seen this?" she whispered. "It's adorable."

It was a clipping from the local newspaper, an article about community policing, and the photograph was of Drew in uniform, grinning beside the open door of his state police cruiser. He looked confident and content, and really adorable.

Throughout the sermon I kept taking the clipping out of my pocket to look at it again. When I got home, I pasted the photograph into the scrapbook Drew and I kept between us.

I still wasn't much for prayer in those days, let alone for traditional "God language," but nevertheless, I scribbled a passionate prayer beneath the picture. *Take care of him, God,* I wrote. *I do love him so much.*

The next morning, Drew's cruiser was struck broadside by a truck fully loaded with ice.

A radio was playing country music, but when one song twanged to its conclusion, the disc jockey paused before beginning the next. There had been an accident on the South

Warren Bridge on Route One, he said, just below Thomaston. Details were sketchy, but it seemed there were two vehicles involved, a box-type truck and a state police cruiser.

I stood at the counter of the Pik Qwik in Thomaston, paying for the gas I had just pumped into my car. Through the plate-glass window I could see my car, where my children waited for me. The Pik Qwik clerk's name is Diane, but she calls herself Hootars, for reasons best known to herself. ("When you buy a lottery ticket from Pik Qwik, Hootars will 'bless it' for you by rubbing it on her breasts," Drew had told me. "There are guys in Thomaston who swear it improves the odds.") When I heard the announcement on the radio station, I turned and met Hootars's compassionate gaze.

"Drive around the corner to the fire station, honey," she said. "They'll know."

The doors of the truck bays at the fire station stood open, and all the bays were empty. I found the dispatcher alone in the office of the deserted building. He turned, saw me, and turned white.

I would not recall, afterward, what I said when the chief of the Thomaston Police rushed from the accident scene to tell me Drew was dead. I remember noticing the bright red of my new bootlaces. I might have screamed, I suppose, or wailed while the dispatcher winced, pinching his lower lip between thumb and forefinger as the rims of his eyes turned red. I don't remember.

What I do remember is that Chief Hosford's face was sad and lovely, and Monica's face shone, transfigured, when she came to me and wrapped her arms around my head as if she could protect me from what had already come to pass. In that moment, I realized that though Drew, my beloved, was lost to me, I was still in love. I was in love with my children, with Monica, with Chief Hosford, with Hootars and Thomaston and all those whom God had placed in my path, and knew I would love and seek only to love with the whole of my broken heart forever.

Chapter Eight

God is love, John's Gospel tells us. That's a whole theology in three words. The practical application of that theology—*God is love*—is nearly as simple. *Be as loving as you can, as often as you can, for as many people as you can, for as long as you live.* Why should you do this? *Because.*

It's simple enough for a child to understand. "I can do it," Peter said stoutly when I explained it to him. "I can be loving toward anyone. Even an ax murderer."

"Start with your sister," I told him.

Start with your spouse. That's what I had to do. Whomever you start with, it doesn't end there. Once I'd gotten the principle more or less down as it applied to Drew, it quickly became obvious that the same could apply to other people, and not just the safely distant murderer who has taken the ax to a stranger. The principle might also apply to the guy who swipes my parking spot at Shop-N-Save, or to the telemarketer who calls at suppertime, or even—imagine this!—*to my relatives!* ("Honor thy father and thy mother," the Bible says, "that thy days may be long upon the land.")

Not long after I was ordained to the professional ministry, Great-Aunt Harriet called to let me know what I would be bringing to her Thanksgiving party.

"Pie, dear," she said. "Any sort. And when we are finished eating, you and I are going to have a *perfectly ghastly argument!*"

"What will we be arguing about?"

"Religion!" Great-Aunt Harriet declared, with anticipatory relish. "Organized religion. It's the worst, the most imbecilic, most *murderous* invention of mankind, worse than the atomic bomb! I shall *dare* you to try to defend it!"

"I see. Well," I said, "it will be a short fight."

The best defense I could offer for organized religion is that it doesn't really *create* human evil; it just gives us another way to justify and express it. Which is pretty lame, and the source is suspect in any case. After all, I work in the bomb factory.

My prosaic spiritual experience didn't actually require me to become a professional minister. Even as a churchgoer, I probably had more friends who did not attend church than friends who did. Unitarian Universalist churches tend to be the last refuge for those unconvinced by dogma, appalled by religious history, and annoyed by the irrationality of religion's claims on our mortal souls.

Every Sunday morning provides the seductive alternative

of a lazy morning spent with coffee and the *New York Times.* Should I be feeling energetic, Maine still offers plenty of enticing options. In the summertime, the warm air and sparkling seas beckon. In the autumn, apples ripen and the forests are radiant. In winter, the sky is clear and the ski slopes are always most perfect (and about 50 percent less crowded, on average) on Sunday mornings.

On such days it seems particularly silly—even to me!—to go to church. Isn't there a kind of spirituality, even a more *authentic* spirituality, something vaguely, yes, wholesomely *Native American* in abandoning the artificial environment of a church sanctuary in favor of, you know, *nature?* All that polished wood, the stained-glass windows—you can't even see the sky from in there! Couldn't one commune with the Divine just as well (or even better?) during a nice sail on the bay, or a hike in the woods, or even a day spent whizzing down the slope at the Camden Snow Bowl?

My friend Elizabeth was, as a child, subjected to a grim form of fundamentalist Christianity. The result is that Elizabeth has a strong, visceral aversion to any and all houses of worship. Although I think Elizabeth might be reasonably comfortable with Unitarian Universalist philosophy, it would be difficult for her to sit in any church long enough to find out.

So although there are plenty of reasons that nice, liberal people don't join churches (statistically speaking, they no longer join the Kiwanis as much as they used to either), my guess is that there are plenty of fine, upstanding people out there who, through exposure to harsh or abusive beliefs and clergy, are not just unchurched but actually *anti*-churched.

No one ever made me go to church, and no one makes me now. I'm a grown-up. Mine is not a belief system in which no-shows are punished with God's eternal pouting resentment. My father was a lapsed Danish Lutheran; Mom a secular WASP agnostic. Our family didn't participate in Organized Religion. This might have been the best thing my parents could have done for a daughter destined for professional ministry. At least my childhood did not predispose me to actually *hate* church.

Still, the fact that I am now so involved in Organized Religion that I ad-minister it to other people does seem to require a positive explanation.

The neuroscientist V. S. Ramachandran asks us to imagine a device, like a sort of helmet, that you could place on your head and stimulate any part of your brain without causing any permanent damage. "What would you use the device for?" he asks.

The device actually exists. A Canadian psychologist used it to stimulate parts of his temporal lobes, and lo and behold, this secular scientist *experienced God* for the first time in his life.

Dr. Ramachandran assures us that this is not altogether surprising. Brain scientists have long noted the connection between religious experience and activity in the temporal lobe. There are even neurological disorders involving seizures of the temporal lobe that result in what is termed "hyper-religiosity." The hyper-religious patient perceives the whole of reality to be suffused with divinity and finds cosmic significance in even trivial events. These patients tend to be loquacious, argumentative; they write to excess, filling journals, writing sermons, maybe penning a memoir or two...um.

Well, okay, but I'm not the only one. The suspiciously prolific writer A. J. Jacobs (raised, as was I, to be a secular humanist) confesses in *The Year of Living Biblically* that, growing up, he too "had a handful of what might qualify as quasimystical experiences. Surprisingly," Jacobs continues, "none involved a bong. They would happen unexpectedly and they would last...about as a long as a sneeze, but they were memorable....I felt at one with the universe. I felt the boundaries of my brain and the rest of the world suddenly dissolve...the glow from these mental orgasms would last several days, making me, at least temporarily, more serene and Buddha-like" (22).

Been there, done that.

When I was seventeen years old and presenting troubling symptoms of some mysterious malady, a neurologist ordered that my head be examined by means of what was then the cutting edge of x-ray technology. A CAT (computerized axial tomography) scan showed a suspicious shadow, a possible lesion—guess where? Smack dab in the middle of my temporal lobe.

I can literally point to the place on the film, the very spot (helpfully marked by the consulting radiologist) that explains *everything.* According to family background and experience, I should be a completely secular humanist, out there skiing, or shopping, or picking apples on a Sunday morning. Instead, I am at church and even in the pulpit! *Because there's something wrong with my brain.*

Dr. Ramachandran, a cheerful Indian American rationalist, is comforting on this score. He, like the neurologist Oliver Sacks, is inclined to find all sorts of creativity and even genius in what otherwise could be considered neurological abnormalities. And who's to say there isn't cosmic significance in trivial events, after all, or that religious traditions have not sprung up precisely to provoke us all into seeing reality as suffused with divinity?

Of course, if stimulating the temporal lobes is really what it all comes down to, it is interesting to imagine what the church of the future might be like. I picture a sanctuary looking like a gigantic beauty parlor, with those electrode helmets hooked to the pews like old-fashioned hair dryers. On my signal from the pulpit, congregants will reverently lower the helmets over their heads, and my job as minister will be to stand there and twiddle the dials. "Oh, dear, Mrs. Sherman needs a little more juice this morning... but whoa! Mr. Trobisch has definitely had enough!"

Before I get too fanciful, I might note that as the mainline Protestant congregations are dwindling, high-tech megachurches are booming. Surround-sound music, PowerPoint presentations, and IMAX film technologies are employed by

American evangelists in their all-out assault on the temporal lobes of the faithful, but before I indulge myself in an intellectually superior sneer, I must point out that the traditional church sanctuary was designed toward the same ends, using the best tools the sixth, twelfth, or nineteenth century had to offer.

While at seminary, I served as student minister to a congregation housed in a lovely, large late-Victorian church in Pittsfield, Maine. It had surround sound in the form of a huge old pipe organ and excellent architectural acoustics. It had richly colored stained-glass windows the size of movie screens, and it had me, occupying the original PowerPoint: a raised candlelit pulpit from which I was to offer inspirational oratory.

That sanctuary was designed to be an enormous neuro-stimulator.

Any religious rite is intended to do pretty much the same thing as the Brain-Helmet: diddle a particular area of the brain—the God Module, if you will—to the exclusion of others, provoking an experience in which all reality is perceived to be suffused with the Divine. So organized religion is indeed intended to be a bona-fide opiate of the people, mind altering in the literal, neurological sense.

Though Native Americans and other aboriginal peoples may have traditionally worshipped *in nature*, they nonetheless did not perform their high rituals casually, in the middle of their daily routines. They too would take themselves as far out of the ordinary human mind-set as time, geography, and/or peyote permitted. At the First Universalist Church of Pittsfield, we did it with stained glass, inclusive-language hymns, and a honking great pipe organ. These were the tools that had been bequeathed to us. Conservative in the classic sense, I personally preferred these tools to a big-screen, computer-animated video drama about the Ascension. Because I am puritanical. I also preferred them to LSD.

The "God Module," when stimulated, makes us deeply feel the awful wonder of being on a level we can only describe as sacred. When our religious feelings are evoked in the presence of others, we may at the same time experience our social connections in cosmic wonderment and awe. We won't retain the feeling—it wears off quickly, as other forms of bliss are wont to do. Still, there is a residue that carries over into the rest of life, strengthening social bonds, building social capital.

Since Americans aren't hunter-gatherers anymore, it could be argued that our society has moved beyond the stage of requiring the sort of social cohesion that religious practice is capable of producing. Organized religion is left to incite mobs and encourage cruelty.

Maybe. Still, I am left with a thought that, though it does not constitute a defense of religion as such, does allow me to continue to work in organized religion with a relatively clear conscience: The fact is that the temporal lobe is, unfortunately, rather promiscuous. It is prone to respond without reference to the reasonableness, morality, or even (strictly speaking) religious content of the stimulus.

First-person accounts of Hitler's ritual-encrusted speeches sound uncomfortably familiar to me. His ecstatic followers too perceived their reality as suffused with divinity and saw cosmic significance in the very being of a leader whose banal viciousness should have been obvious but, catastrophically, was not.

"A man will worship something," Ralph Waldo Emerson declared. We've all got temporal lobes, though some are less excitable than others. So the question is not "Will we worship?" but "*What* will we worship...today?" If everyone who considers herself too reasonable and rational decides to abandon organized religion altogether, who will be left to provide stimulation to the temporal lobes of the masses, at least some of whom are, as I am, neurologically predisposed for religious experience?

Short of adjusting the human genome or performing wholesale neurosurgery on the populace, *a [hu]man will worship something.* Who will name and refine the interpretive boundaries of her synaptic exaltation? Will that someone or something provide a better, more wholesome outlet for the ecstatic overflow of our all-too-human temporal lobes than organized religion has? Will that alternative have the social, historical, and perhaps even neuroanatomical reach it needs to prick my conscience and fire my sense of justice, and—most important—will whatever else we come up with be immune to the failures of religion?

I don't find the history of our twentieth-century experiments with alternatives particularly encouraging. But maybe

I am wrong. It is certainly possible that love *isn't* the most important thing in human life. Even if it is, something other than my relatively traditional religious practice might very well do a better job of making me more open to love, more generous, and more inclined to serve. God knows, churches fail, and I fail at love with embarrassing frequency, especially given that my whole life is supposed to be consciously bent to that single principle. Yet there it is. And here I am, my head with its defective temporal lobe bent down before my folded, tainted hands, praying. In church.

Chapter Nine

In secular psychology, it is understood that the ability of an adult to exercise executive control over her own behavior, defer gratification, and conform appropriately to social norms depends heavily on the quality of parenting she or he received as a child.

As I learned in my seminary classes, it is likewise well established in *pastoral* psychology that children's understanding and acceptance of the metaphorical Divine Parent is deeply rooted in the care they received from their actual mother and father. For example, a young person whose father was harsh, abusive, or sexually exploitative is unlikely to hear the words "our Father, who art in heaven" in quite the same way that Zach, Peter, Ellie, and Woolie did after their father died. When they heard the Lord's Prayer, they pictured their dad patrolling the skies, still clad in his state police blue uniform, now neatly tailored to accommodate wings.

After 9/11, my daughter Ellie said she imagined all those

who had to leap from the terrible, flame-filled windows at the World Trade Center landing safely in her father's outstretched arms. *Hallowed be thy name...*

My own father "art in heaven" also, as of the summer of 1997. A mere twist of the mental lens and there he is, clad in his omnipresent pale blue oxford shirt, grinning down at me from some comfortable cloud. His cowlick stands up on the crown of his head, and he pauses in the middle of striking a match to wave his pipe at me, generating a characteristic shower of fragrant tobacco.

"Kate-O!" he barks. "Kate-O, the chop-chop here in heaven is just *terrific!*"

Dad wasn't a perfect father. For one thing, as a foreign correspondent for the *New York Times* and later, in Vietnam, for the *Washington Post*, he was gone for weeks, months, even a whole year at a time. He had an explosive and unpredictable temper, an inborn trait (after all, I inherited it) doubtless exacerbated by the stresses of his job and, arguably, by the residual effects of having served as a United States marine in Korea. He was badly wounded when a grenade exploded in his foxhole, and it is virtually certain that Dad's psyche sustained injuries also, whether or not these were ever named as, for instance, post-traumatic stress disorder. After all, a human nervous system can only take so much, and Dad was a human being.

So Dad had a temper, and he and I had our conflicts, some hurtful. Still, Dad was what Bruno Bettelheim called "a good enough" parent.

* * *

I have a young friend who as valedictorian gave a speech at the graduation of his costly boarding school. His mother, a single mother of three, sat in the front row all dressed up, proud as could be of her fine boy.

His speech was titled "My Family." The gist of it was that the family was an outdated, patriarchal, and even imperialist institution doomed to be abolished when the Revolution finally gets here. In the meantime, he for one had realized that the instructor of everything good and noble in his character, the source of all that was truly nourishing, his only true family, was...

Are you ready for this?

Pink Floyd.

His mother's face went blank when she heard it, not so much from shock as from confusion. She thought Pink Floyd was a brand of bathroom cleanser. This, fortunately, muddled the issue long enough for her to get through the remainder of the speech without quite realizing that her son was dissing her.

My adolescent friend did not realize his tirade renouncing ties of blood and nurture had an ancient antecedent. In a story common to the Gospels of Mark and Matthew, we find Jesus surrounded, as usual, by throngs of admirers clamoring for his attention. Jesus is holding forth, as he wont to do, about various interesting subjects: unclean spirits, sea monsters, how a house that is divided against itself cannot stand ("Ooh, that's a good line, eh? They'll remember that one!").

And while he was still speaking to the crowds, "his mother and brothers came and, standing outside the house, they sent word to him, wanting to speak to him. Someone told him 'Look, your mother and your brothers and sisters are outside, waiting to speak with you.' And Jesus replied, 'Who are my mother, my brothers? Whoever does the will of God is my brother and sister and mother!'"

At least as far as we can discern from the Gospels, Jesus never does invite his mom in, doesn't let her sit down for a little while, have a cool drink, be introduced to his friends. We don't actually hear about Mother Mary again, in fact, until—loyal to the end, in spite of the way her son dismissed her—she's standing at the foot of the cross.

Jesus was many good things, no doubt, but he wasn't a good son.

Maybe he was a nice baby. Maybe he slept through the night like a little lamb, right from the start. But I doubt it. I'll bet he had colic. I'll bet he screamed like a little banshee, and older women would come over to the stable, cluck their tongues, tell Mary she was just too tense, she needed to relax a little, her milk was bitter, maybe she should cut down on the caffeine...

There's an interesting extracanonical Gospel called the Infancy Gospel of Thomas that discusses Jesus' childhood in depth. I recommend this Gospel to anyone laboring under the misapprehension that the early Christians, by choosing a mere four out of the dozens of Gospels then extant were somehow suppressing vital spiritual truths. The Infancy Gospel of Thomas is really awful.

Its author had obviously read Luke. The narrative neatly fills in the gap that occurs in Luke between the nativity in the stable and the moment Jesus reappears as a twelve-year-old, wowing the elders in the Jerusalem temple with his preternatural discernment while his mother searches frantically for him through the streets of the city. The Infancy Gospel serves as a sort of prequel, but in it Jesus is a nasty little monster. He knocks some kids off a roof, and slays birds with his word. When another kid doesn't get out of Jesus' way fast enough, Jesus zaps him dead. The parents, understandably upset, come around to see Joseph. They tell him he's got to get this rotten kid under control before he kills every kid in the neighborhood.

Can you imagine what Christianity might have looked like if the early editors of the New Testament decided to include this gem in the official Word of God? Christian history might have been...well, it might have been even worse! Still, even from the evidence available to us in the officially sanctioned stories, Jesus may not be a homicidal brat, but he is awfully hard on his mom. He takes her for granted. He dismisses her. He ignores her. He uses her as a foil for his own wit.

Why is it so difficult to recognize your own mother as a human being? One day, not so long ago, my mother called. It had been a bad day. My kids were driving me nuts. I was glad to have an ear to complain to, so I complained. "My kids are driving me nuts!" I told her. "They ignore me. They take me for granted. They dismiss me. They don't seem to realize that I am a human being."

"I know. I know," my mother said.

After a while, we said good-bye and hung up.

A few minutes later, I realized that during that whole hour-long conversation, I hadn't once asked my mother how she was, or what she was doing, whether she'd read any good books lately, even.

Mother's Day was begun by Unitarians. In my denomination, we're pretty proud of that. It was conceived, moreover, not as a sentimental holiday involving breakfast in bed and a bouquet, but rather as a day of universal ceasefire that should be observed by every side in every war then raging. It was said that in this way, the mothers of the world would have a respite, if only for one day, of fearing their sons would die on the battlefield. Unitarians get quite high-minded about this, and it is commonly proclaimed from Unitarian Universalist pulpits on Mother's Day that we should return to the original antiwar meaning of the holiday. Which is okay, but we should remember that the original Mother's Day wasn't really about mothers any more than Luke's nativity was about Mary. Both were really about the sons.

Mother's Day is now a retail opportunity. Purveyors of everything from garden tools to diamonds proclaim that an expensive consumer item is just the thing to make Mom forget all the ways in which you disregard her. My siblings and I would bring home objets d'art produced more economically at school under the tender tutelage of teachers who assumed we had the sort of mother who wanted sweet framed handprints, or paper flowers, or maybe an apron edged in rickrack, laboriously sewn in home ec.

My mother was not that sort of mother.

My mother is a small woman with a sort of silver afro of curly hair. She's very smart, and rather eccentric. Right now, for example, my mother lives in a farmhouse in Maryland with seven dogs, innumerable cats, a couple of orphaned deer, and more than two hundred exotic birds. Finches, parakeets, lorikeets, cockatoos, canaries, African gray parrots, a macaw...rooms that used to be bedrooms and living areas are now completely taken over by birds in cages and birds on stands. If you call my mother on the telephone, you can hear them all squawing and hooting and chirping in the background. She's got a parrot that sings opera and one that mimics her voice so perfectly that my mother speaks in stereo: "Hello?" *Hello? Hello? Hello?*

This is the sort of mother one's friends find fascinating, but it isn't a proper sort of mother.

Maybe Mary was an interesting, improper mother? We know she was unorthodox. She was pregnant by God at an early age; what did she have to lose by being eccentric to boot? Maybe she had artsy friends and odd hobbies?

Mother? said Jesus. I have no mother. *Pink Floyd is my mother.*

*   *   *

So why do I still need to call my mother when I am sad? Why does just the sound of her voice—even duplicated by that stupid parrot—make me feel, even in dark moments, as if everything might just be okay after all?

We are told, in the Gospels of Mark and Matthew, that Jesus' last words were *My God, my God, why have you forsaken me?* It's a line from Psalm 21, and it is certainly possible that these would be among the words an observant Jew might utter at such a moment. But then, Mark and Matthew agreed, he cried again, "with a loud voice," and breathed his last.

What did he say, in that loud voice?

In moments of dire pain and peril, on battlefields, for instance, the dying man's last utterance is nearly always the same as his first. *Mama,* he will say. *Mama.*

It is the easiest syllable to form with the human mouth, the sound that names the first touch of love; it is the original prayer and the ultimate prayer: alpha and omega, beginning and end. *Mama!* A prayer for comfort, for milk, for mercy.

Mary, standing off at a little distance from the cross upon which her son had been hung, could not answer him. She could be there, as she had always been there, living her hard, human life alongside him as he lived his, but she could not save him. She was only a human being. Why is that so hard to remember?

The summer after Drew died, sometime in June or so, I was having a particularly hard time. I was confused and lonesome. I was afraid. I picked up the telephone and dialed my mother's number. "Mom," I said. "I am confused and lonesome. I am afraid."

"I'll be right there," she said.

I'll be right there... I'll be right there, said the parrot.

I picked her up at the airport. I'd brought us a couple of coffee Coolatas for the car ride home and was sipping mine when Mom appeared at the baggage claim. There she was, my interesting little mother, standing beside the luggage carousel, with bird feathers in her silver afro. She was wearing a heavy canvas vest. The vest was filthy. It looked as if my mother had been standing under a tree full of pigeons for about three days.

"Mom," I said, handing her a Coolata. "What's with the vest?"

"This vest?" Mom said, looking down at herself. "I love this vest. It's my special traveling vest. It has so many useful pockets."

"It's covered with bird poop."

"Is it? That's odd. I just washed it last week."

"It's disgusting."

"But it has all these useful pockets..."

"Jeez, Mom, you're hopeless," I said, with a short laugh.

I didn't say it to anyone else. The acolytes waiting for me to spin amusement or wisdom from this moment at my mother's expense were, for the time being anyway, imaginary. I rolled my eyes heavenward—who is my mother?—and lifted my cup to take a long, superior sip of my Coolata.

I had forgotten about the straw. When I raised the cup to my face, the plastic straw went up my nose. It went quite far up my nose, in fact, and it hurt. A lot.

"Oh, honey-bunny!" said Mom.

I put the cup down. I withdrew the straw from my left sinus cavity. I gazed at my first God, my mother—my stubborn, interesting, improper mother, this human being living her life alongside mine.

"Thank you for coming, Mom," I said. "I'm so glad to see you. Have you read any good books lately?"

Chapter Ten

I like this definition of *love,* or *caritas:* "to earnestly desire the achievement of wholeness by the beloved." Notice that it doesn't say, "To give the gift of wholeness to the beloved" or "To impose wholeness on the beloved." This can be hard to remember when it comes to one's own children, who are, as Kahlil Gibran said, "the sons and daughters of life's longing for itself." Kahlil Gibran didn't actually have any children, incidentally; he just wrote lovely things about them.

"How do you do it all?" a woman who doesn't know me asked when she heard that in addition to being a law enforcement chaplain and a writer, I am mother to six children (including steps).

"I do quite a lot of it badly," I said.

If you are intent on becoming a truly loving person, learn to apologize. Love means having to say you're sorry over, and over, and over ...

At about the age of four, my daughter Woolie learned to cuss and write. Graffiti began to appear around the house: *DAM!* it said. *DAM!* written in crayon on the hall wallpaper. *DAM!* written in Sharpie on the bathroom floor. *DAM!* written in blue chalk on one of the ceiling beams in the kitchen.

"Woolie!" I bellowed upon discovery of this latest outrage. "Come here right now!"

Woolie appeared in the kitchen doorway. Reading my expression, she offered her most disarming smile and burbled, "I yuv you, Mama."

Fixing my daughter with a withering glare, I pointed in silent accusation at the blue chalk on the beam. Woolie craned her little neck and surveyed the damage.

"I din' do dat."

"Woolie, sweetie, you have to stop writing bad words on the walls," I said. "Writing is for *paper* and bad words are for..."

"For Mama!" Woolie concluded confidently.

"No! Not for... well, for grown-ups. Bad words are for *grown-ups* in *extreme* circumstances..."

"Okay."

"Do you understand me? No more!"

"Okay, Mama," Woolie agreed. "But"—she pointed her small pink forefinger at the profanity on the beam—"I din' do dat."

"Woolie!" I cried. "A lie just compounds the sin!"

"I din' do..."

Just then it occurred to me that Woolie probably hadn't.

Not because the child was too virtuous, but because she was too short. There was no way, even standing on the tallest kitchen stool, that Woolie could have reached that kitchen beam. This meant the true culprit could only be...

"*PETER!*"

The name Mary is spoken with reverence in our house. No, not the Virgin, and not the Magdalene. The Mary we speak of is Aunt Mary, Drew's sister, a superb and beautiful human being whose soft, sweet southern drawl conceals (though not for long) a delightfully ribald sense of humor. Zach, Peter, Ellie, and Woolie have made a pilgrimage to Georgia every summer to get in touch with their southern roots and, not incidentally, to experience an enchanted few weeks of truly top-drawer parenting courtesy of Aunt Mary and Uncle Jeff.

Aunt Mary takes my children to Six Flags over Georgia, where instead of squatting resentfully in the dusty grass, complaining about the heat, she actually goes on the rides with them. Aunt Mary gets their hair cut at a real hairdresser's for an annual professional correction of their mother's home hacking. Aunt Mary plays with my children in the swimming pool instead of sitting on a chaise by the water with her nose in a book, and Aunt Mary gets my children the sugary cereal they crave. She lets them eat it in her bed while watching cartoons. And Aunt Mary snuggles in there and watches the cartoons with them.

I don't own a television. If I am in a particularly indulgent mood my children might be permitted Raisin Bran instead of plain bran for breakfast. Still, Mary insists I am good mother. "Y'all are much better at discipline," she points out.

"Maybe," I answer doubtfully. Her own two children grew up to be delightful adults, so as mothering goes, it's difficult to see how the Mary Method (*gratia gratis data*, "grace freely given") is in any way inferior to the Kate Method ("Life is a coal mine, children...").

When my children compare me unfavorably with their beloved aunt, I point out that I am the one who lets them visit her. Have I not, in fact, made sure over the years that they would have plenty of quality time with Mary and her family, with their grandparents, with my brother, CP, and my sister, Angelica, and with many other indulgent friends and kin? True, ruthlessly exploiting these relationships allowed me to complete a master's degree and start a career in ministry, but I'd like to think it was a win-win deal, at least for me and mine. Spending time with other adults expanded my children's knowledge of the world (Grits! Shopping malls! *Survivor!*) and of the various ways life is lived and love expressed.

I also hoped—or rather, prayed, with the ardor of the novice—that the protection and regard generous friends and dear relations offered to my children might fortify their soft and all-deserving hearts against the results of their mother's inevitable failures.

"I try. And I hope I never let you down too badly," I told each child. "But listen, beloved: If there ever comes a time when you need help and Mama is not paying attention... then for God's sake, keep going. To Aunt Mary, or Uncle CP, or

Tonya, or Monica, or Tom. Keep going, and *keep telling,* until someone hears you and responds."

Of all the endearments and embraces, all the expressions of my passionate affection and admiration for them, I still think this was one of the best things I ever said to my children, or could have.

Peter appeared by my bedside one morning. Grinning, he had both hands hidden behind his back, and his blue-green eyes were lively with expectation.

"CELEBRATE MOM!" he crowed joyfully, and flung two enormous handfuls of flower petals into the air. They were very pretty as they fell across the white bedspread in their brilliant shades of ruby, rose, and cherry red. My boy had gotten up early and gone around the house and systematically denuded my geraniums of every single blossom then extant. The stains they left on the white bedspread would prove irremediable. For months to come, I would find single flower petals and damp, moldering clumps of flower petals everywhere: in my bed, in my hair, in my shoes, in the pockets of my bathrobe, and—mysteriously—twined in the entrails of dust bunnies as far away as the second-floor linen closet.

"Oh, Peter," I said gratefully. "Thank you."

CHAPTER ELEVEN

It was early December, and snow was falling. The white pines in the backyard looked as if they had been draped in lace. A fragrant fire blazed in the woodstove, and Nat King Cole crooned carols. Sipping hot chocolate, I was already in my usual holiday mood, one composed in roughly equal parts of panic, resentment, and self-pity.

I had planned to knit or otherwise handcraft all of the presents for my children, nieces, and nephews. That was back in August, when time had seemed limitless. Now Christmas loomed, and my nephew Bagna was the only one likely to receive a handknit sweater. Admittedly, it was a beauty, knit in intense shades of red and gold, but it wasn't finished. *Bagna already has a lot of sweaters*, I told myself. *Maybe this can be a vest if there's no time to knit sleeves.*

I was hemmed in on all sides by shopping bags spilling over with things that had now to be wrapped, boxed, taped, addressed, and—because many of my relatives live far away—mailed.

How many forests fall for the sake of silly wrapping paper; how many barrels of crude oil are sacrificed to make plastic tape? I wondered grimly. And all to wrap presents for children who need or want for *nothing*. All these things will have to be cleaned and stored and fussed with. At great cost in time, money, and earth's finite natural resources, I would be sending my dear little loved ones clutter! Wrapped in trash!

"Why don't we just cut the forests down, suck the oil out of the ground, and burn it all directly?" I inquired aloud. "Why take the unnecessary step of making clutter and trash out of them in between?"

"Yes, yes," my children said soothingly. They were bent over letters to Santa, missives filled with the details of their consumerist desire. Only Ellie conscientiously asked after the fat man's health.

Speaking of fat, there are feasts to shop for and treats to prepare. "And how," I wailed to my sleek, well-nourished offspring, "am I to create meals symbolic of abundance when every meal is abundant, every American mouthful a confection of exotic ingredients hitherto known only to kings?"

"Yes, yes," the children said, but indistinctly, through mouthfuls of chocolate, butter cookies, and peppermints.

Next year will be different, I vowed. I would make more contributions to causes. I would donate my handmade sweaters to the truly chilly poor. Surely I could teach my kids to give and accept gifts of effort and thought without all the cardboard boxes, wads of crumpled gift wrap, and those infernal packing peanuts that would litter the floor on Christmas Day? *Dear Santa: Could you please, please just put an extra five bucks in the Salvation Army bucket for me and call it good?*

Next year, I decided, *I'll simplify.*

For the time being, however, like most other Americans, it was too late: I had overindulged, overfed, overspent, and overstimulated. Among the most cosseted people ever to live on this planet, my family and I could anticipate a day in which we would give and receive yet more. And, of all things, I was feeling sorry for myself.

Pity the one who has never known hunger. From him has been withheld the meaning of food.

By my own standards I have been "poor," but by historical and global standards I have never been anything other than fabulously wealthy. The Muslim prophet Muhammad invited all his followers, but especially the wealthy ones, to a ritual fast. Fasting would offer the good Muslim a taste of poverty and inspiration to give more generously, but fasting would also permit her to truly experience the wonders of the feast.

I'm not a Muslim. I don't fast, and dosing myself and my family with guilt amid the pleasures of the holiday season seems uncomfortably akin to serving up a little wedge of lemon to cleanse our palates between courses.

*   *   *

When I was eighteen, I developed a string of mysterious neurological symptoms. After assorted tests (including the CAT scan, which revealed that interesting lesion on my temporal lobe) I was diagnosed with multiple sclerosis.

A disease of the central nervous system, multiple sclerosis, or MS, results in a gradual deterioration of function, resulting eventually in paraplegia, quadriplegia, and even death.

The diagnosis was wrong—I did not have MS—but the diagnosis stuck for nearly two years. During this time, I went to MS doctors and MS support groups and took MS medications. I had MS restrictions imposed on my imagined future. Whatever I planned, whatever I might once have hoped to accomplish, I was now convinced that mine would be a foreshortened life of progressive disability. But then I was rediagnosed.

Now, I wasn't cured. I never had MS to begin with, and whatever had been the cause of my symptoms had disappeared without leaving a calling card. To this day, no one knows what was wrong with me. (Lyme? Delayed adolescence? Religiosity?) Whatever it was, it was gone. I was healthy. I didn't have MS and I still don't.

I don't have cancer either. (Not yet, anyway.) I don't have diabetes. My leg isn't broken, I'm not blind, and no bombs have fallen on my house. My children are alive and healthy. All of these are facts and they are gifts. I can thank God-from-Whom-All-Blessings-Flow as glibly as the next person, but the one gift I remain grateful for to the marrow of my bones is this one: *I don't have MS.*

More good news: I have a nephew named Bagna. He is a lot of fun to knit for. His espresso-colored skin stands up beautifully to bright colors that look ghastly on my pasty Caucasian relatives.

Think of the poor, God tells us, and not just the *poor in spirit* (a category in which I, prone to self-pity, am apt to include myself) but the *actual* poor, the ones who yearn for *caritas* in the form of food, warmth, or safety—for Holy love in its simplest, most basic form. While many messages in the Christian Bible are ambiguous, or open to debate, this one is asserted as God's unqualified, clear command: that we should give concrete assistance *to the poor.*

My brother, CP, offered his concrete assistance in Togo, West Africa, while serving with the Peace Corps. As CP was finishing up his sojourn there, Bagna's parents, residents of the village where CP was stationed, came to him with what seemed an odd request. Would CP please adopt Bagna and take him to America?

"America is very far away," my brother told them. "If I took Bagna with me, the chances are good you would never see your little boy again."

"Bagna will die if he stays in Togo," Bagna's mother said. Indeed, Bagna had already been very ill, more than once, and probably would not have survived thus far had my brother not been there to purchase the necessary antibiotics. Once CP left the country, there would be no one to buy the medicine.

"How about if I send you money?" CP asked. "You can use it to buy milk for Bagna, and medicine if he needs it?"

The answer was no. Bagna's parents explained: That wasn't how their village society worked. Such a gift could not be wasted on a child, particularly a frail one. Any money that came into their village had to be spent on adults. It sounds heartless, but when times are tough, folks don't invest in children. You can make more children. Children soak up resources and time and produce little, if anything, for the good of the group. So poor families and poor communities tend to invest in those who are capable of producing food or earning money, and the kids get what is left over. In Bagna's family, what was left over was not enough.

If Bagna did not go home to America with CP, he would almost certainly have become one of the millions of children throughout the world and across the millennia who would not live to see his fifth birthday. That's just the way things are.

In Roman-occupied Palestine around the year 1, this is the way things were: Unhealthy, unwanted, or embarrassing infants were routinely left at the dump with the kitchen scraps. Out of this culture came a story about a baby born one cold night to a young woman espoused to a carpenter.

A star shone like a jewel in the night sky above this infant's birthplace, and wealthy, wise men came to him, bearing rich gifts. What an absurd tale this must have seemed to its earliest listeners—kings traveling far to kneel beside a cradle, offering their wealth to a baby? Get real! Why would wise men risk their gifts? Wouldn't they know that half such babies die? And Jesus wasn't even a royal baby, a prince, but an ordinary child and one, if we may say so, of rather dubious paternity.

Later in the same story, the adult Jesus startled his disciples when he told them, "Suffer the little children to come unto me." His disciples balked: Were these weak, useless beings, occupiers of the lowest possible rung of society, really to be brought into the presence of the Messiah, there to be dandled, fed, and blessed? "Suffer the little children to come unto me," Jesus insisted. And oh, little children do suffer, don't they?

When I was first diagnosed with MS, I asked, "Why me?"

The inescapable answer was *Why not me?* Who among the people offering brave camaraderie at those MS support group meetings actually deserve this pitiless disease?

Then I was rediagnosed. I was healthy, and the same question had to be asked. *Why me?*

Bagna came to America as a runty three-year-old with a big belly. He had six different kinds of intestinal parasites, endemic malaria, rotten teeth, and the quiet nature of a child enervated by constant pain.

In his new life with my brother, Bagna had all the miracles my brother was eager to provide: access to antibiotics, milk, fruit, plenty of protein, and a good dentist. He had books, clean bathrooms, good schools, an auntie who knits, and a fine dad with energy and devotion to lavish on a small boy.

Why Bagna?

Why not Bagna?

There are so many reasons for me to be grateful at Christmas or in any season: I don't have MS. I do have a nephew named Bagna, a skinny little boy who grew into a strapping, intelligent, handsome American man, a graduate of Williams College now exploring the mysteries of high finance in his first job on Wall Street.

Monarchs should be brought to their knees before the miracle of every human life. The star of abundance, grace, and health should shine above every cradle. It should. But it does not. Still, that star doubtless shines on the children you know, as it has shone so generously on my children, Bagna included. *Fall on your knees; hear the angel voices:* In our absurd abundance, my brother was able to offer what millions of generations have longed for. *Rejoice, rejoice...* Among all of our other gifts, we have more than we need and our children are warm. Their bellies are full, and we can afford to behold them. We can afford to love them.

CHAPTER TWELVE

Woolie and her friend Madeline kindly kept me company on a working weekend in Bar Harbor. While I gave a speech about law enforcement and religion to a convention of municipal administrators, the girls explored the town's shopping district, where lobster-themed T-shirts, humorous refrigerator magnets, and other essential tourist items could be found in staggering abundance. We met back up for supper.

The waiter flirted with them, bringing them complimentary seconds on their Shirley Temples. Woolie tied the stem of her maraschino cherry into a knot with her tongue. That night, we slept in a hotel. Or at least I did.

Loud whispers and scufflings roused me at two in the morning. "Wooooolie...?" I whined. "Jeez, are you girls still awake?"

"We're writing letters to the people down the hall," said my daughter importantly.

"You're writing...?"

"They're having a lovers' spat!" said Madeline.

"The lady's name is Angela and the man's name is Jason," Woolie confirmed.

"You can hear every single word they say!"

"She doesn't like it that he wore running shoes with his nice pants, and he thinks she should admit that the bartender in the hotel bar used to be her boyfriend."

"We're giving them advice. I'm writing my letter to Jason," said Madeline. Her tongue protruded from the corner of her mouth. "I'm telling him it isn't helpful to use obscenities."

"Angela needs to let Jason finish his sentences," said Woolie. "How do you spell *harangue?*"

I pulled the pillow over my head and went back to sleep. Woolie and Madeline finished their letters, decorated the margins of the paper with drawings of flowers and birds, and, strenuously shushing each other, tiptoed down the hall to slide them under the combatants' door. This charitable deed accomplished, they crept out the back door, climbed over the barrier fence, and took an illicit swim in the hotel pool. The next morning I found their underpants, soggy and reeking of chlorine, on the carpet right next to my bed.

"I wonder if it stopped the fight?" Monica said when I told her about Woolie and Madeline's impromptu marital intervention.

"I would imagine they quieted down anyway," I said. "People generally behave better when they know there are witnesses."

In fact, it wouldn't surprise me to learn that Woolie and

Madeline made a real difference in how Jason and Angela interacted with each other, at least for that day or even longer. Misbehavior and abuse thrive on isolation and anonymity. This is true for wife-beaters, but it is also true for the rest of us who succumb to the distressingly common temptation to treat our loved ones as punching bags, figuratively if not literally.

What would happen if, on hearing my neighbors shouting at each other, I suddenly discovered an urgent need for an egg and dashed over to their house to borrow one? I suppose it's possible that I might innocently walk into a situation so dire that my personal safety was at risk...but I doubt it. And I suppose it's also possible that I could interrupt just at that magical moment when one partner was about to utter the one remark, the single obscenity that would have lanced the boil of their rage, clarified all the issues, changed the dynamic, redeemed the union...if only I hadn't stuck my nose in. Yeah. Maybe.

A couple was having a nasty spat in public one day when I happened by, but we were on a city street, which can seem almost like privacy. Passersby were edging around them, eyes averted, and why not? It was none of our business.

The young man was shouting; the young woman screeched a tearful *contrapunto*. Between them, a small child sat glumly in a double stroller, eating Cheerios out of a plastic bag. An infant dangled, drooling, from the crook of the young woman's arm, and her little fat legs flopped back and forth with the force of her mother's flouncing. As I edged past, I turned my head just in time to see the young man draw back his boot.

"And you did *what?*" said Trooper Tom Ballard when I told him this story.

"I, um, leaped between them."

"Are you *nuts?*"

"He was going to kick her!" I protested. "There was a baby!"

"What if he had kicked you? What if he had had a weapon? *Jesus,* Kate!" Tom spluttered. "Do you know how many cops get killed intervening in domestic violence situations?"

"Of course I know! But there was a *baby!*"

As it turned out, I didn't get kicked, shot, or stabbed. While wincing businessmen and homeless people passed us by, I stood on the sidewalk between husband and wife, gabbling witlessly: *You don't really want to kick her... You don't want the baby to get hurt... There are other ways of handling this... Do you by any chance have a religious tradition we could draw upon here? How do you feel about Jesus?* The young woman took the opportunity to kick viciously at her husband's ankles from behind the shield I had provided her. *That's not helpful, young lady... Shall we call your pastor? The crisis hotline? How about your mom?... I mean it, honey, knock that off... Is this what you want your children to live with? How about a prayer?*

In the end, the man and woman were united by, if nothing else, their shared dislike of this creepy, relentless religious lady. They calmed down and departed peacefully enough, their children safe for the moment at least. I have no idea whether I did a good thing or a foolish thing, whether my action made things better in the long run, or worse. Maybe it had no effect at all. The baby, whose extreme vulnerability prompted my action, would now be in grade school. Are her parents still together? Still fighting? I'll never know.

I do know this, though: A certain cherrywood coffee table would still grace my home had if only a neighbor had shown up, babbling about Jesus and requesting an egg.

I went to a Catholic university Back in the Reagan era, when I prided myself on being a left-wing radical atheist. You didn't have to work very hard to be thought of as left-wing at Georgetown in those days. Most of us on the student left were really just Democrats with hairy armpits.

But there weren't many of us, even at that, so although I was officially Ms. Campus Feminist, I was once called on to pinch-hit for Mr. Nuclear Freeze, who had been slated to debate a member of Georgetown's thriving colony of Young Americans for Freedom on the campus radio station. He came down with the flu, and I went to the radio station in his stead.

The debate began with the student talk show host asking us both what we thought of the morality of deploying the Pershing missiles in Europe. The Pershings were widely considered to be offensive weapons to be used in a nuclear first strike against the then–Soviet Union. I, naturally, took the position that any nuclear first strike against Soviet cities was morally wrong. The Young American for Freedom simply dismissed the question. "Morality," he said coldly, "has nothing to do with war."

Needless to say, the conversation degraded swiftly into a violent argument, which terminated when yours truly uttered a glass-shattering shriek that echoed across the campus airways:

"Excuse me, but *do you believe in Jesus Christ?*"

The Young American for Freedom sneered. "No."

"How can I talk to you?" I said, and stormed out in tears.

It was an absurd little tempest in a small teapot, but what made it even more ridiculous was that *I didn't believe in Jesus Christ!* I was a left-wing radical atheist! It was hard to explain to all my radical secular friends what exactly had caused me to lose my mind as well as the debate.

As a post-Christian, left-leaning, nondoctrinal, noncreedal Unitarian Universalist, I don't have to believe in Jesus Christ if I don't want to. Okay, UUs don't reject Jesus—we are tolerant people who try not to reject anyone. Still, inclusivity and tolerance are time-consuming; there are a lot of religious sources to be mined for wisdom, all sorts of scriptures to serve as subjects for our sermons and sparks for our spiritual ecstasy. So Unitarian Universalists can theoretically avoid what an old Jesuit professor of mine used to call the Problem of Christ.

Still (though it seems rude to point this out), at my

church in Rockland, we don't dress up, buy lilies, or eat lamb (or tofamb) and jelly beans, and we don't pack the pews on Rosh Hashanah, Eid, or Buddha's birthday. Easter, the day that Jesus of Nazareth, having been tortured, executed, and entombed, is said to have come back to human life, remains a holy day for most of us.

I went to a Catholic college and a Christian seminary. The Bangor Seminary's professor of philosophy was Dr. Oscar Remick. A native of Ellsworth, he had a distinguished career teaching at various elite institutions before returning home to Maine.

Diminutive, spry, always impeccable in a crisp white shirt and tie, Oscar hopped and chirped before the class like a grasshopper surrounded by so much lush green grass. He was the kind of teacher who when asked a truly stupid question (and yes, there is such a thing) would congratulate his interlocutor without a hint of irony and use the question to launch the class into an illuminating discussion.

Oscar had studied under luminaries of liberal Christian thought back in the 1950s, when these were still the stuff of mainstream intellectual conversation. My mother even remembers going to hear the theologian Paul Tillich lecture at Harvard in 1959, although, owing to Tillich's German accent, Mom didn't understand a word.

Oscar studied with Tillich at Union Theological Seminary, as it happened, and while explaining one or another of Tillich's more complex ideas, he would do a comical imitation of Paul Tillich's glutinous Teutonic baritone.

"Trrrransparency! *Yahwol?*" he would rumble. "*Achtung! Das saints, holy men, der Bible, these are not the Ultimate! Dey are transparent to the uuultimate! Yahwol?*"

Um…

"Okay," Oscar continued in his normal voice, "I'll illustrate." He folded his arms across his starched shirtfront and scowled thoughtfully for a few moments. Then he brightened: "Ah! Imagine that a friend has come to visit my wife and me at our home in Ellsworth. Yes? The friend arrives, we offer a cocktail, some canapés, and then, quite naturally, we stroll over to the big picture windows that make up most of the living room wall. 'What a beautiful view,' my guest might say.

" 'What is it you see?' I ask her. I should tell you parenthetically, so to speak, that our house is right on the water. *Marvelous* setting—it's why we bought the house. So how might she answer?"

"Um… 'I see water'?" ventured someone.

"Yes! Brilliant! 'I see water,' she says. Anything else?"

Rocks… seagulls… seaweed… clouds… Oscar beams at us; we're so clever, we're wonderful students and fine human beings! "Splendid! Yes. But now, my friends, do you know what she *doesn't* say? My guest does not say 'I see a big pane of glass.'"

Dramatic pause.

"The glass is what is closest to her eyes, isn't it? If you look at a window, you can generally see the glass, unless it is very, very clean. So why doesn't my guest say 'I see glass'?"

"Because the glass is transparent," someone said.

"Exactly! Yes! Yes! The whole point of a window is that you look *through it*. Right? If she were to say 'I see the windowpane,' we would think she was silly: The whole purpose and function of a window is to look through it, to see what lies beyond it."

"Ahhhh," said the class.

"Ahhhh, indeed! Yes, my clever friends, this is what Tillich was trying to get at: Scripture is a window. A prayer is a window. The Bible is a window and even—though Tillich got in trouble for saying so—*Jesus was a window*."

"Wait a minute," someone said. "I thought Jesus was the view."

"Perhaps. Perhaps," said Oscar judiciously. "But it is interesting to read through the Gospels after reading Tillich and notice how Jesus himself keeps directing the disciples' attention beyond himself, directing his own prayers and assigning his many miracles beyond himself to God. Jesus himself seems to confront that maddening human tendency to look at the glass, to worship the pane, so to speak, instead of the view."

This idea was disquieting to many of the Christian students in Oscar's class. I loved it. The notion that Jesus was an Atoning Sacrifice for the Sins of Mankind never struck much of a chord with me, but Jesus as a window? That I could work with.

"Okay, but if Jesus was a window, Jesus was a *special* window," the student persisted.

"Of course," said Oscar, nodding. "Of course. Very special. Though I should mention that toward the end of his life, Tillich was investigating other religions, particularly Buddhism. Had he lived, he might eventually have been willing to countenance the possibility that *Jesus was one of several special windows,* unusual perhaps, but not unique."

My immediate spiritual ancestors—the Unitarians, the Universalists—saw God through Jesus: They were Christians. Still, when I asked that conservative Republican boy back at Georgetown whether he believed in Jesus Christ, I wasn't trying to shift the conversation to theology, a subject about which I knew even less at the time than I did about nuclear weapons policy. I was, rather, searching for a point of shared perspective, a window, you might say, that we could gaze through together and discuss the common view.

But even if that pompous young YAFF-er had confessed faith in Jesus Christ, the conversation might still have abruptly ended: It is so depressingly common for that which reveals to be thickened and dulled by use and abuse to become opaque. Tillich himself acknowledged that transparency isn't permanent. In fact, the quickest way to ruin a window is to worship it; to make the Word, the Book, the human being, into an idol, to abandon the view and focus on the glass.

Christian windows prove opaque to many these days, encrusted as they are by so many centuries of humid idolatry, and it can be hard to get excited about the Risen Christ, reentombed as he has been by so many layers of hypocrisy and bigotry. People might be forgiven for going in search of new windows, *post-Christian* windows, to gaze through. If you are included in this group, I have perfect faith that other windows will have opened to the view. It is a glorious view.

Still, I will confess it: Though for many, Jesus has become impervious to light, the stories of Jesus told in the Gospels retain their transparency for me. Jesus was a human being, a man of flesh loved in flesh by his companions and his students in all the ways we love the mortal: deeply... bravely... foolishly. For the end is always death, and this is hard.

Weeping, Jesus' friend Mary went to sit beside his tomb. This was all that had been left to her of loving this man, and it was not so much to ask, was it? That she be allowed to sink down before her lost beloved's resting place and cry for a day, or a year, or forever... But Mary found the tomb open, empty, and surrounded by strangers.

"Whom do you seek?" one of these asked her.

"What do you see?" My teacher Oscar inquired of his guest. *Water, birds, the sky...*

Oh, but Mary wants Jesus, her human friend, her beloved teacher, the man with whom she had had a real relationship, voice to ear, smile to smile, skin to skin. Of course she wants him back. But Jesus is dead. And gone. *Please,* she asks. *Please give him back to me.*

"Mary," Jesus says to her.

She turned and said to him, in Hebrew, "Rabboni!"

The way the Christian promise is generally interpreted, Mary doesn't have to be sad anymore because Jesus isn't dead anymore. Nice, eh? Who wouldn't want *resurrection* to mean that those we have loved and lost are restored to our embrace?

But Mary can't embrace Jesus. *Do not cling to me,* he says.

So what was true for me and true for you remained true for Mary Magdalene, even after she learned how to love him, even after his resurrection from the dead: We can't have our dear dead ones back, not as they were, not as we loved them. It isn't the beloved that resurrects. It's love itself.

CHAPTER THIRTEEN

So a priest and a nun—call them Father John and Sister Mary-Margaret—are heading from Milwaukee to Baltimore on some ecclesiastical mission or other when their car breaks down. The closest garage can repair the car, but Father John and Sister Mary-Margaret will have to spend the night in a motel and—wouldn't you know it?—the local Days Inn only has one room available.

Still, the room comes with two beds. So Sister Mary-Margaret and Father John agree to take the room for the night, and after eating an adequate supper at a nearby diner and watching the news on TV, they get into their pajamas and lie down in their separate beds. Father John switches off the bedside light.

A few minutes go by. Then Sister Mary-Margaret speaks. "Do you find it awfully chilly in here, Father John? I just can't seem to get warm."

"Maybe you need another blanket, Sister?" Father John climbs out of bed. He fetches an extra blanket from the closet and brings it over to Sister Mary-Margaret, covers her up, and gets back into his own bed.

A few more minutes pass. Then: "Um...Father? I'm terribly sorry, but I'm just so cold. What might really warm me up, I wonder?"

Father John gets up. He fetches another blanket from the closet, spreads it over Sister Mary-Margaret, and again gets back into his bed.

A few minutes more minutes and Sister Mary-Margaret pipes up yet again: "Oh, Father...I can't imagine what is going on with me, but I'm still shivering; my body just can't seem to get warm all by itself..."

Father John sighs deeply. "You know, Sister Mary-Margaret," he says, "I've been thinking."

"Yes, Father?"

"You and I are all alone in this motel room."

"Yes, we are."

"No one in Baltimore knows we're here together. No one in Milwaukee knows. No one at the diocese knows, and in fact, no one will ever need to know what happens between us tonight in this room..."

"True, Father."

"So I was thinking maybe...just this once, Sister...you and I could act as if we were *married*..."

"Oh, Father!" Sister Mary-Margaret breathes.

"That is, would you enjoy it, Mary-Margaret, if I behaved, just for tonight, as if I were your husband and you were my wife?"

"Yes, John! Yes!"

"Fine," said Father John. "So get your own goddamned blanket."

Rudeness and indifference will kill a marriage. Infidelity will do it too.

My former boyfriend found it incomprehensible that I steadfastly refused to grant my blessing to his departure from our shared life. If I had truly loved him, if I was a truly loving person, even—and didn't I always claim to be this?—shouldn't I be happy for him, thrilled that he had at last found true love in the arms of another?

I tried to explain: "Only a masochist goes around saying 'Ah, yes, *of course* your happiness is worth my pain'!"

"What about Jesus?" my boyfriend asked with a sneer.

This was the boyfriend I had during the interregnum between my first husband and my second. Though we did not wed, each of us had made representations regarding the durability of our union not only to each other but to Zach, Peter, Ellie, and Woolie, and to our friends and family members.

So the end of that relationship was something akin to a divorce even though neither church nor state was involved. When the boyfriend announced he had been seeing another woman, I was presented with a problem no amount of talk, patience, or prayer could fix. So I did what people generally do in response to this particular provocation: I lost weight. I stopped sleeping. I walked around struggling to breathe, as if I had a strap buckled tightly around my rib cage. It was awful to suffer this on my own account, but worse to have to accept that I was helpless to protect my children from more loss, from yet more suffering.

And in general, I discovered, people don't bring casseroles when you break up.

"He'd better not try fishing without a license, is all I can say…" Jesse Gillespie growled comfortingly, and in certain circles, it was declared that Kate's now ex-boyfriend should likewise avoid exceeding the speed limit, allowing his inspection sticker to expire, and all similar behaviors that might bring him to the attention of a Maine state trooper. My civilian friends were satisfactorily partisan too. "That *fucking* bastard!" Monica declared. "What are you going to *do?*"

What was there to do? I ordered a complete set of DVDs of *The Mary Tyler Moore Show* from Netflix, and the kids and I sat on the couch and watched them back to back for days. We ate macaroni and cheese. I knit several thousand useless woolen hats. Everyone's grades slumped—including mine, at seminary. Everyone cried, though Zach, seventeen, and trying nobly to be man of the house (again), did his best to hide it. Peter experimented with the anesthetic properties of Pabst Blue Ribbon at a party and was brought home by the Thomaston police. Ellie was superbly indignant, but Woolie got really depressed, enough to scare me. So I plucked her out of school one day to go in search of the sole remedy my mother insisted would cure her.

The Braestrup tradition has always been to adopt strays from the Humane Society when canine companionship is called for, but this was an emergency. At Petland in the Topsham Fair Mall, sharing a clean glass tank with a narcoleptic Daschund, a Jack Russell terrier puppy the size of a gerbil caught Woolie's eye. The saleslady scooped him up and placed him in Woolie's arms for a trial embrace.

I inspected the price tag. "Oh my God," I said.

The puppy licked Woolie's cheek and widdled. My daughter turned her desolate eyes to me and smiled a small, watery smile. I bowed my head and laid my money down.

Woolie named the puppy Chaos. He was a huge hit with the whole family. Even our old blind collie-retriever mix, Lassie, recovered enough joie de vivre to play with him. "You know what this reminds me of? A bumper sticker," Tonya said when she came over to watch *Mary Tyler Moore* with us. "I GOT A DOG FOR MY BOYFRIEND. BEST TRADE I EVER MADE."

Love is all around . . . you're gonna make it after all.

Chapter Fourteen

The adrenaline of the day had worn off. I was pooped and weepy, and not just because the day had been difficult. I was still suffering aftershocks from the recent demise of my relationship. So as I waited for the gas station's owner to fill the tank of my car (grateful that I had at least managed to find a full-service gas station), I assured myself that I would never permit anyone to become Significant to me ever again.

In fact, I decided, at the earliest opportunity I would join a convent. Chastity and poverty had the inestimable advantage of being honest and clear, compared to the veiled, swindling sacrifices of your average Meaningful Relationship. In the cloister, surely, I would find a balm for my hurts, nectar for my sore and thirsty heart. In a community of seekers committed to the simple purity of love, the abundance of love could only be such that I would be able to lavish it upon the world and never feel—as I felt at that moment—as if I were running dry.

The gas pump gurgled and stopped pumping. The tank was full, but the owner didn't reappear. I waited for a few moments, then got out of the car, replaced the nozzle in its cradle, and went to find him.

He was on the telephone in the gas station's tiny office, and he held up his index finger apologetically as I entered. As he talked into the phone, he eyed my clothing. I wore my green uniform jacket with Maine Warden Service patches and a badge. The knees of my black uniform pants were dirty, and my boots left gritty crusts of dried mud on his floor. Reading the job description written in bold red letters above my left breast, the owner brought his phone conversation to a close and hung up.

"Chaplain, eh?"

"Yup," I replied.

"For the wardens...huh."

I braced myself for the inevitable *What does a warden service chaplain do? Bless the moose?* Instead he continued, "Y'know, I thought I heard the warden service went along to that plane crash over in Winthrop today. Were you involved with that?"

"We were there." I handed him my state-issued gas card. "The state police actually investigate plane crashes, but the Warden Service was called because it was in the woods."

"It sounded like a real bad one," the owner said, and I nodded but didn't offer details. He wouldn't want to hear the details. "I fly," he went on. "That is, I'm a pilot, which is why I paid particular attention when it came on the radio. Terrible."

"It was."

"I don't want to crash, but I've always had a dread of falling out of an airplane. You know? Like from thirty thousand feet."

"That would be pretty dreadful."

"I hear you do stay conscious the whole way down too. So you know what's happening but there's nothing you can do. Well," he conceded, with a vague gesture toward the clerical collar around my neck, "you can pray, I guess. But it's not like God's going to stick a big hand out of the clouds and catch you."

"I wouldn't count on it." I signed the receipt for my gas.

"Which is the thing," the owner said. "I mean, if you're falling out of an airplane, you know you're all done."

"Yes," I said.

The man was still holding my credit card in his fingers, tapping the edge of it against his other palm as he composed his thoughts. "I know you're never supposed to give up hope. If you have faith in God, right?" He gave my clerical collar another significant look. I started to reply, but he shook his head.

"When my wife was dying of cancer," he continued, "her church kept praying for a miracle, right up to the end." He waved the credit card. "The day she died, that exact morning, the minister visited, and I told him the doctor had been in and my wife was going to die. So I told Pastor Mark, and you know what he said? He said, 'Son, don't give up hope.'"

"Really?" I said. I kept my voice carefully neutral.

"Didn't let me finish the sentence, even. Jumped right in with that. 'Son, don't give up hope. We're all praying for a miracle—don't give up hope.'"

I met his gaze. "I would guess that wasn't very helpful," I said thoughtfully.

"Not at all. Not at all! It made me feel bad, like...like if I said she was going to die, she would die."

"You didn't need that."

He coughed, handed me my credit card, and turned his attention to the task of peeling the yellow portion of the receipt from the white one. He handed the yellow one to me. "I don't go to church anymore," he said. "No offense."

"None taken," I said.

I took a long while filing the receipt away in my bag, as if it had to go in just the right place. "You know," I said at last, "if you are falling out of an airplane, there's no hope."

"Not without a parachute," he agreed.

"So if you're falling out of an airplane, there's no hope to give up. No one is going to suspend the laws of gravity. As you say, God isn't going to stick a giant hand out of the clouds and catch you."

"Nope."

"I wonder if there could be something sort of liberating about that?"

"Liberating?" He thought about it.

"If there's nothing you can do, there's nothing you *should* do."

"People couldn't expect a lot from a person," he conceded. "Under those circumstances."

"Exactly. So if there's no hope...then all that's left is curiosity."

"Huh." The gas station owner scratched gently under his eyebrow with a greasy thumbnail. "You mean, like, *Gee, so this is what it's like to be falling thirty thousand feet?*"

"It could be interesting...if you decided to take an interest."

"Maybe falling feels like flying?"

"If I ever fall out of an airplane, I hope I remember to be curious. Since it's my last adventure, I hope I actually pay attention."

"If I ever fall out of an airplane," the gas station owner said, "I hope I remember to do a few backflips on the way down!"

I laughed appreciatively, and the gas station gave my uniformed shoulder a shy sort of comradely smack. Then we said good night and I drove home to my children, and to my solitary bed.

Hopeless, I sighed to myself as I prepared for a night of restless, unsatisfying sleep. I was brushing my teeth and thinking of my love life.

Still, I thought, *it would be sort of nice to have someone fall beside me for a while.*

I got into bed. *Not to cling to, mind you, not to use as a parachute either. It would be nice to have a hand to link my hand with as we flip and tumble, hopeless, through the unmoved sky.*

*   *   *

It is my job to love Maine's game wardens; that is to say, to *earnestly desire their achievement of wholeness.* It occurred to me the other day that my theology is not only simple: It is tautological. (Isn't that true of all the best and most successful dogmas?) When someone achieves perfect wholeness, he or she will by definition also be perfectly loving.

My smug satisfaction at this orderly construal lasted only until I realized that the more you love, the more capacity for pain you shall also bear, for as the man sang, love hurts. To the extent that I (lovingly) assist game wardens in maintaining or increasing their capacity for *caritas*, I shall also be maintaining or even increasing their vulnerability to pain.

Damn.

"If I died, would you remarry?"

It's time to discuss line-of-duty death at the Maine Criminal Justice Academy. We have already gone over the various policies and procedures the Maine Warden Service has in place, each one introduced with my fervent variations on the theme of "God forbid, but if…" My job consists in part of leading discussions about such things at the academy.

I've done a fair imitation of myself as a young law enforcement "A-unit," as spouses are called: initiating pillow talk, posing the question in an elaborately casual tone, with a careless giggle thrown in for good measure. "Y'know…*tee-hee!* Would you, like, find a new wife?"

They groan appreciatively. It's the kind of question that

anyone who has been married for any length of time can recognize as prelude to a brouhaha, whether the questioner actively intends to provoke a fight or not.

Drew gave the best possible answer, and not only because, being soft, it neatly turned away wrath. "You might want to write this down," I say, and give the wardens his answer, word for word.

"'I don't know,' he said seriously. 'But I do know that if I were to die first, I would want you to remarry. I wouldn't want you to have to go through life alone.'"

"*Ohhh,*" the older wardens chorus. (The dude was *good!*)

I know a widow whose husband, also a state trooper (though not from Maine), was killed in an accident not long after they had had this common little conversation. "Baby, if you marry some other guy, I'm gonna come back and haunt you!" was his answer. I'm sure it was uttered at least half in jest. It was certainly spoken out of perfect ignorance: He was young. He had never been widowed. *He didn't know.* As it turned out, the poor guy did end up haunting his widow, at least in a sense. Her first, tentative steps out of the unfathomable loneliness he had not been able to imagine had to be made in defiance, and therefore resentfully.

One February day, a late-winter sun shone brilliantly, and in my snowpants and parka I was warm enough to flop down in a snowbank, turn my face to the sky, and bask. (Later, I would find I'd gotten a sunburn.)

I was in no particular hurry for one of the search boats

to detach itself from the flotilla of boats out on the sparkling surface of the lake and come ashore to fetch me. I had a lot to think about.

On the previous afternoon, Monica had called to ask if I happened to remember meeting a friend of hers, a man named Simon, at the Winter Festival in Camden.

"Should I?"

"He's handsome."

"Oh," I said.

"According to him, the two of you spoke briefly at a funeral last month too. You made a big impression on him," she went on.

"I spoke to a lot of people at that funeral," I said.

"I know. The important thing is that Simon remembers you." Monica said this in an alarmingly meaningful way. "And I think he's great, Kate. I really like him, but I wanted to check and make sure it was all right with you before I gave him your phone number."

By the light of a waning moon, a thirty-two-year-old man rode his snowmobile into open water. People have been known to survive such errors with life, limb, and even snowmobile intact, but there's only one way to do it. The moment you identify as liquid the black expanse gleaming beyond the edge of the ice, you have to open up the throttle and drive your snowmobile as fast and straight as you can, right out across the water. If you turn, and the edge of a ski tips under the surface, the snowmobile is going to flip and go down.

If you allow your speed to drop, the forward thrust of the churning caterpillar track behind your seat will not be equal to the weight of the chassis, and you will sink.

One snowmobile actually made it across this very water just that way: straight and fast. Just up the beach from where I am basking, a set of tracks declare the place where, after traveling more than a mile and a half across moonlit water, this unnatural amphibian craft arrived back on solid ground. That driver was experienced, and fortunate. His friend was neither.

"We've got the sled," Warden Jeremy Judd announced by way of a greeting as his boat's bow at last crunched gently into the cold pebbles at the water's edge. He stepped overboard and waded the last few feet ashore and pulled the boat up to where I could clamber aboard without getting my feet wet. Captain Joel Wilkinson, the dive team leader, had sent Jeremy ashore to fetch another oxygen tank, some food, and, incidentally, the chaplain. "It's right off the edge of the ice shelf, just in front of where some skid marks show where he tried to jam on the breaks and turn. Mistake number one," Jeremy said.

"How about the body?" I asked.

"Nope. And the water is really clear: You can look right down and read the registration sticker on the console. But no sign of him, and we've been diving pendulum sweeps all around the sled for an hour."

"Huh," I said. A lifeless human body does not ordinarily stay on the surface. Absent the buoyancy of inflated lungs or a life jacket, gravity wins as gravity will and the body descends until it finds solid ground, but once it is there, it generally doesn't move much. Even a fairly strong current won't push it far. (This made more sense to me once I learned to think of the body as a one- or two-hundred-pound solid object.)

On the other hand, if the victim did not drown but expired of a heart attack, his lungs might have stayed inflated enough to hold him on the surface. But Jeremy looked skeptical. "He was only thirty-something," he said. "Family says his health was good. Joel thinks maybe he didn't take off his helmet or open the visor. That would be mistake number two. So if he actually drowned when the helmet filled with water, there might have been enough air trapped in the top of the helmet to let him float for a bit. There was a strong wind last night. And right to the south of the place we found the sled, the bottom slopes off and then just drops away. Joel says if he went down in that deep part, he could be under two hundred feet of water. If that's the case, we might never find him." This had happened before. We both remembered that snowmobiler, drowned in this very lake. By all evidence, his body remained beneath two hundred and fifty feet of cold water, while his widow and daughter had to go on without him and without either his salary or life insurance, which wouldn't be paid until the body was found or five years had elapsed, whichever came first.

By this standard, today's drowning victim's family was in luck: On the second pass, with the second team of divers,

Warden Bruce Loring, who was handling the communications gear, held up his hand to quiet the group on the dive boat. "Scotty has him."

The drowned man's wife had eyes so brown they are almost black. Would I commend her husband to the hands of God? she asked me. Would I do this as soon as his body was recovered? He was a good husband, she wanted God to know. "Can you say my name?" she asked. "My name is Anita. A-N-I-T-A. Can you tell God I loved him?"

It works this way sometimes: People look at me in my clerical collar and see a consul, someone who can send a dispatch straight to heaven as if by diplomatic pouch. "Of course I can."

"God already knows, prolly."

I hoped my smile looked like sympathy, because what I was feeling, more than anything, was admiration. Her little hands trembled, and her knees were shaking under the thin stretch fabric of her sweatpants, but she said she didn't need to sit down. She had been pacing, and would keep pacing until the wardens and I returned to confirm the news. "God probably does know," I agreed. "But I'll remind him."

Scott came to the surface, his arm wrapped around the dead man's chest. Jeremy rummaged in one of the storage compartments for a body bag. We all helped to hoist the body over the gunwale of the dive boat. Scott found the camera and took photographs for the record. When everyone was ready, I knelt down on the boat deck beside the body, laid my hand on the hard, cold forehead, and whispered to God of Anita's love.

Anita can sit down now that her loss has been confirmed. She can rest now that she is no longer obliged to hope, I thought. Finished praying, I dug the zipper pulls out of the plastic seams with cold, clumsy fingers and carefully zipped the bag around the body while Joel started the engine. Then I clambered up to sit beside Jeremy in the bow of the dive boat.

I know, I thought. *In fact, I know too much. I know too well. When I forget, I am reminded. If Monica's friend Simon calls this evening, after this day, I probably will have to tell him no.*

Jeremy and I were quiet until we were almost at the landing. We listened to the glassy shattering of shell ice as the dive boat made its way back across the refreezing lake surface to the shore.

Don't be an idiot, Kate, Drew said.

Jeremy stretched his neck, rolled his shoulders, cleared his throat, and asked if I would marry him. He was tall, sweet-tempered, prone to blushing, and he was looking mighty fine in his neoprene dive suit.

"Yes," I told him.

"Oh, boy!" said Jeremy, his eyes shining, his cheeks scarlet. "Wait'll I tell Melanie!"

CHAPTER FIFTEEN

There are Persons of God who offer truly heroic *caritas* to the homeless and to the inhabitants of lunatic asylums and prisons. They brave the unsanitary and olfactorily offensive abodes of the ignorant and impoverished, and risk moral as well as physical peril serving alongside our armed forces.

Others serve in houses of worship, bearing quotidian witness to the workings of God. For those brave souls, there are budgets to oversee, politics to manage, and meetings to attend, not to mention the weekly requirement that they say something both entertaining and spiritually coherent from the pulpit.

Meanwhile, I've got the best ministry job you can imagine. I hang around with good men, and with citizens who are generally decent people, even if they might be disoriented, hypothermic, injured, or grief-stricken. I get to spend a lot of time outdoors, in various picturesque Maine locales. My ministry involves few meetings and little to no paperwork. How did I happen upon such a ministry?

Well, I live in Maine, which not only boasts scenery but also a convenient and excellent seminary. As a law-enforcement widow, I was *well positioned,* as they say, to be considered when the position of Maine Warden Service chaplain opened up. Because Drew left me with a pension and health insurance, I could afford to start out as a volunteer. I had family and friends to help me rear my children, so I was able to devote time and energy to my work.

"How did you get into this job?" Monica's friend Simon asks me over coffee on our first date.

God placed it in my path.

"Can you tell that joke at the wedding?" Jeremy asked enthusiastically of the "get your own goddamned blanket" story, and Melanie swats him. "What? It's religious!"

"The more usual readings are from First Corinthians 13, or the Gospel story of the Wedding at Cana." Jeremy and his fiancée, Melanie, have come to visit me in my office in Augusta. "I recommend taking a little peek at the Song of Solomon, and of course you may have favorite verses or poems you'd prefer." I hand them a selection of wedding readings. We discuss the location for the ceremony, the order of service, the number of bridesmaids and groomsmen, the flavor of the cake, and whether an iPod can be programmed to provide music for the processional and recessional.

"What about vows?" asked Melanie. She's an attractive, intelligent young woman with a beautiful smile. She looks undersize, though, and I can't tell whether this is because she reminds me of the widow Anita or if it's just because any normal person looks like a elf standing next to Jeremy.

"Well," I said, "you've got a few choices. There are the traditional love-honor-and-cherish vows, which come in a few versions…" I hand them a sheet of paper. "There are less traditional vows…" (more paper) "…and of course you could…ahhh…write your own."

I've heard people stand together before God and solemnly promise to make the coffee every morning, vow to never go to bed mad. I have also heard couples, bowing to what they imagine to be the dictates of realism, promise only to remain married *so long as love shall last.*

Traditional vows are not what a cynic might call realistic, but neither are they romantic poetry. The vows are rather an articulation of that stern dimension of love that is not feeling but *decision.* "You aren't really promising to *feel* love," I told Jeremy and Melanie with approval—they've gone with traditional vows. "You are promising to *do* love."

To love, honor, and cherish a fresh, productive, and attractive partner is easy. That's when it's morning coffee, chocolate at Valentine's Day, and if you go to bed mad, what the hell: It just adds a little *frisson* to the evening's activities. But when your partner is discouraged, unemployed, or injured, when he or she has Alzheimer's and can't remember your name, then loving, honoring, and cherishing will need to find alternative modes of expression. "But it's still loving, honoring, and cherishing," I said. "The words are elastic enough to cover everything from your first dance together to your first day in Depends."

"And you want us to actually say 'till death do us part'?" Melanie asked carefully.

It was hard not to picture Anita's dark eyes, her brave mouth as she asked me to pray for her husband. "Look at it this way," I said. "Being parted by death is actually your best-case scenario. Being parted by death is what happens *if a marriage works.*"

"Wow," said Melanie. "*Wow.*"

"I never thought of it that way," said Jeremy.

"So," I said cheerfully. "where are you going for your honeymoon?"

They left my office looking sober, even a little stunned.

What luck or fate or divine decree brought the game warden Jeremy Judd and his beloved Melanie, a dispatcher for the town of Windham's municipal police department, together? Well, once upon a time, Melanie was the dispatcher during a chase Jeremy was involved in... and what a romantic story we can make from this: Our hero 2123 is out there, driving code 3 through the valley of the shadow of darkness, but he shall fear no 10-50 or 10-74, for a lovely voice is with him, filtering steadily through the static on the statewide car-to-car channel... And by the time the chase is over, Warden Judd knows, deep in his heart, that he has to find the owner of that voice and make her his A-unit, mother to all his little B-units...

Except that when they did meet up after the chase back at Windham P D, they realized it wasn't actually the first time they'd met. Warden Judd and Melanie had their first date in the eighth grade, and their first kiss too. Okay, so this could be a good, romantic story too...until you remember what eighth-graders are like. Adolescence is not the most attractive, discerning, or physically coordinated time of life—trust me on this: I have teenagers at home. How good a kisser could Jeremy really have been, at thirteen?

"I guess he was good enough," said Jeremy's colleague Jesse, wriggling his eyebrows at me, and I laughed.

Jesse reminds me a little of my boy Peter: There's red in his hair, and he feels things fiercely. One autumn day, he pointed out a monarch flittering its way across the vast surface of Sebago Lake. It was headed south, Jesse said, showing me his compass to prove it, presumably embarked on the butterflies' annual migration to Mexico. "They have to fly so far on those little wings. It's all I can do not to scoop 'em up and carry them south in my truck," he said. "Poor little guys. Hell, I could get 'em as far as Portland, anyway."

To my born-again friend and occasional confessor Pastor Moira, I admitted I was having a few uncharitable thoughts about Jesse's wife, Georgina.

"But who knows what this guy is *really* like?" Moira said, clearly intended it as a rhetorical question.

"I've spent a lot of time with him," I said stubbornly.

Moira sighed. "Sister, all I'm saying is that you're biased when it comes to game wardens, and you might as well admit it."

"I admit it," I said.

In some ways, I am as automatically protective of the game wardens as I am of my children. Once, for instance, the *Lewiston Sun-Journal* ran an article about the investigation of a family's supply of (poached) deer meat and illustrated it with a crude editorial cartoon depicting a game warden dressed to resemble a member of the Gestapo. Shocked, Colonel Santaguida showed the cartoon to me, but he was temporarily distracted from his own outrage by the spectacle of a chaplain in an incandescent fury: hair standing on end, flames shooting from my eyes, my voice an unnatural *basso profundo: Don't mess with my babies!*

"What is the plan for your daughter if the two of you split up?" I asked Jesse.

Jesse pushed up the bill of his ball cap and brushed a weary hand across his forehead. "Daycare," he said. He pulled the cap back down, and the brim fitted itself neatly into the pink wrinkle it had already etched in his brow. "We can't afford to run two households on my salary, and Georgina wants to get out of the house. I can't really blame her for that. Georgina had a lot more fun before she was a mother—she was really lively, really popular, always had a lot of friends around and things to do. Then we moved to the woods, and now she has a toddler to chase after. Well, you know. You've been there."

I asked Jesse if Georgina might be persuaded to try marriage counseling, if only for little Molly's sake. "A divorce puts any kid into a statistical risk category for various significant tribulations," I said carefully. "It's an argument for taking things slowly."

"She says Molly will be happy if her parents are happy. She doesn't want to spend time and money listening to some guy who just wants to scare her, and convince her to stay with me."

Might she come by my office in Augusta just to talk?

"I don't know," Jesse said. "She likes you. She's always telling me I should spend more time with you, although I think she means it as an insult."

"You mean, that you're in need of divine intervention?"

"Yeah. But she likes you for real too," he said again, thinking aloud.

"I like her," I said. Which was true: Georgina was a cutie. I had taken to her immediately when I met her at a department function some months back.

Still, there was a time when I would not have had much sympathy for Georgina. With puritanical certainty, I would have declared that all marriages save the violent were salvageable and should be salvaged, especially if there are children involved. My marriage, after all, had definitely seemed headed for divorce at one time, and didn't the redemption of that union represent my life's greatest spiritual and moral accomplishment thus far? So, though I tried to approach conversations about divorce with humility, in truth I was sure that my own experience was—or ought to be—universal.

My parents separated in the 1970s, a decade in which laws governing divorce and the attitudes of helping professionals changed rapidly and radically. Divorce became both common and acceptable. This was seen as a necessary and even a positive thing, liberating, in fact, especially for women. Psychologists had begun to downplay the negative impact divorce might have on children, declaring that divorce per se could be neutral or even good for children.

The context our society creates for us has always influenced, even delimitated the possibilities for any given relationship. If in what my children call the Olden Days death caused broken, mended, and reblended families, we now live in what Barbara Dafoe Whitehead has called a divorce culture.

When my parents first discussed their divorce with their children, a full year of legal separation was still required before a divorce could be finalized. Within that first, mandatory year, in fact, my parents reunited. Many years, and many iterations of the separation/reunion cycle later, they finally divorced for good.

It isn't up to me to say either that my parents' divorce need never have happened, or that it would have been better had the proceedings been completed and finalized two months after my mother first broke the news to me.

For one thing, qualitative terms such as *better* and *worse* would have to be defined. You get married "for better or worse," but in theory, you get divorced only because it's supposed to make life better. But how much better? In the long run or in the short run? And the question would have to be reconsidered for each individual involved—my mother, my father, each of my siblings. Then there's the community in general, which declared itself to be an interested party when it placed its social, historical, and legal imprimatur on the relationship back at the start. Was the community better off with my parents apart, and if so, how much weight should that carry?

I, for one, considered my parents' impending divorce a dire calamity. This was true even before I had experienced the concomitant changes that separation and divorce commonly bring into the lives of children. We moved (yet again), I changed schools (yet again), money became distinctly tighter, and I think it is safe to say that both my mother and my father were distracted from their parental roles by the intensity of their own feelings and adjustments. This is inevitable. It happens after a spouse's death too—I certainly was not at my best, parenting-wise, when first widowed. (But people brought casseroles.)

Aside from the happy fact that I was now free to love and marry someone more agreeable, the not-quite-a-divorce from my boyfriend proved distinctly useful to me as a minister. It let me catch a glimpse, at least, of what happens when a marriage simply falls apart.

If my ex-boyfriend and I had lived a hundred years earlier, we would have been married, not living in sin, and arguably, everyone and everything in our social environment would have conspired to keep us married. Perhaps the end result would have been tolerable; the relationship could have been "saved," as my relationship with Drew was saved (and, if I may say so, proved salvific). But we don't live a hundred years ago. We live now, in this culture, the one in which people do set up housekeeping and even go on to bear young out of wedlock, the one in which sex has no culturally inescapable connection to commitment, the one in which freedom and privacy are valued much more highly than duty and community obligation. Whether we like it or not (and, let's face it: for the most part we do like it), this is the world we are in, the world in which my parents tried and failed (and tried again, bless them, and failed again) to remain married, the world of Jesse and Georgina, Jeremy and Melanie, my ex-boyfriend and his true love and…what were their names, the couple who received impromptu advice from two adolescent girls in a Bar Harbor hotel? Never mind.…It's their world, too.

This is the terrain we stumble across, bearing our fragile hearts in our clumsy human hands. It's a brave thing, to try to love, but then, it always has been.

When I called my father in Washington, DC, to tell him his son-in-law had been killed in a car accident, "I'll be right there" was all he said, and he was.

He walked through my front door in Maine at three thirty in the afternoon, perhaps four hours after the phone call, six hours after Drew's death. The entirety of his focus, my stepmother later told me, had been on getting to Maine. He could not seem to speak, she said, so that she had some trouble finding out from him what had happened and to whom. Yet when my father stopped at the Avis counter at the Portland Jetport to rent a car, he also reserved one for my mother, knowing she would be coming along behind him.

Chapter Sixteen

In the summer of 1997, the kids and I accompanied Dad to Denmark for a family reunion. American and Danish Braestrups met in the seaside town of Rorvig for a blissful month of shared meals, celebrations, expeditions to castles and museums, and days spent with first, second, and third cousins cavorting on a glorious white sand beach ("Naked!" Woolie remembers gleefully) and swimming in the cold blue Scandinavian sea.

Dad and I had long vowed to make a pilgrimage to the Navel of the Universe, the town of Braedstrup (the original spelling includes a *d*) whence the original Ancestor was born and raised before migrating to Copenhagen in the seventeenth century. "You will know why the ancestor left," my Danish cousin Bo predicted grimly. "It is so boring!" Nonetheless, with as much ceremony as we could extract from the occasion, Dad and I set off.

Braedstrup is located more or less in the middle of

Jutland, the big fat "hand" portion of the Danish mitten that is separated from the "thumb" (where Copenhagen and Rorvig are) by a strip of sea. This we crossed on a clean and speedy car ferry that boasted, among its manifold amenities, an elegant restaurant (with a wine list) and a room full of computers, so that passengers, duly mellowed by *fiskebolle* and Beaujolais, could surf the Web for Scandinavian porn.

Back on the mainland, I drove along through a gentle summer landscape of fields in shades of green, with occasional, enlivening patches of yellow where a fallow field had been allowed to rest under a vivid coverlet of rape (*Brassicaceanapus*). I told Dad about the visit the children and I had made to the local Danish police station the day before. "The police station was very clean—"

"Of course," said Dad. "This is *Denmark*."

"—and quiet. The walls were painted in cheery pastels and hung with tasteful paintings of nudes."

Some pipe smoke went down the wrong way and Dad experienced a fit of coughing. "Female nudes?" he growled hopefully once he had recovered.

"Both, Dad." I smirked. "This is Denmark."

Dad rolled his eyes and relit his pipe, flapping his hands ineffectually at the smoke. I glared at him and opened my window.

"OOOOOH!" Dad shouted suddenly. "Stop the car! *Stop the car!*" Startled, I pulled onto the shoulder. I scanned wildly around, trying to pinpoint the threat. "Look at that!" Dad gestured dramatically with the stem of his pipe. It was a road sign:

BRAEDSTRUP
80 KILOMETRES

Dad insisted I get out of the car and be photographed in a rapturous pose beside the road sign as mystified Danish motorists slowed and gawked. "Hold still," he barked. "Stop smirking!"

Back in the moving car, Dad kept his head out the window. He inhaled deeply, claiming the air was growing noticeably fresher and sweeter. Then, "STOP!" he shouted again, and with that same, unsettling suddenness.

BRAEDSTRUP
70 KILOMETRES

"Now where the *hell* did I put my camera?"

"Oh, for God's sake," I protested, but Dad insisted.

In Denmark, as in other civilized nations, road signs appear at predictable intervals all along the roadways. So, in answer to the obvious question, yes there does indeed exist a series of photographs of yours truly posed like a conqueror in front of the signs that marked our progress in ten-kilometer increments all the way to Braedstrup.

At last, a mere five kilometers away ("Just smell that air!" Dad said, clicking furiously away with his camera), we reached a rest stop. I went into the bathroom while Dad pressed a fresh wad of tobacco into his pipe and gravely examined the laminated tourist map that stood beside the parking lot.

"They call this the Hill Country of Denmark," Dad announced when I emerged. We looked around but didn't see anything we would term a hill, exactly. Still, these things are relative, and Dad was pleased to add "hills" to the list of good things Braedstrup was known for.

"Do you want to use the toilet while we're here, Dad?" I asked him. "It's very clean."

"I'm sure it is," said Dad dreamily, "but I'm saving it . . . saving everything for Braedstrup."

We laughed so hard at this, my Dad and I, that we had to cling to each other, convulsed by sheer, sobbing glee. It was the best moment of the whole, great trip: laughing that hard, with Dad.

A month later, trying not to look at the heart monitor suspended above his bed, I held Dad's hand in a hospital emergency room and jabbered about our trip to Braedstrup. I talked about the buns we bought at the Braesdtrup bakery, the daytime drunks we met at the Braedstrup Bar, the dignified photographic portraits we importuned strangers to snap of the two American Braestrups in front of the Braedstrup laundromat and the Braedstrup Equestrian Supply . . . Behind his oxygen mask, Dad grinned.

"Don't forget to call Sandy," he said. "Give her my love."

"I'll take care of it, Dad," I said.

The nurse injected some more morphine into his intravenous line. "It's for the pain," she explained. "And it's also a thrombolytic."

"A clot-buster," I told Dad.

"The nurses here are just ter-RIF-fic!" Dad said. His eyes closed as the drug reached his brain. His mouth worked behind the mask.

"The medicine makes your mouth dry," the nurse reassured him. "Don't worry. We'll get you some water in a little while." Dad struggled to keep his eyes open.

"It's all right, Dad," I said, squeezing his big hand gently in both of mine. "I'm right here. You can let go." Dad nodded again. He let his eyes close, and his brow cleared. And then my father died.

One hundred percent of marriages end. As long as we're being brutally realistic, however, why not admit the whole truth? *One hundred percent of all relationships end:* paternal, maternal, spousal, avuncular, friendly, or filial; one way or another, you will lose everyone you love, everyone you cannot bear to lose.

One response to this appalling reality is to posit the existence of heaven, a place where everyone gets to be together again, just like the old days (though, as my friend Moira declares, in heaven her husband is going to fold laundry).

In the meantime, however, what are those of us still here on earth to do in the face of loss? Jesus has some advice: When he is no longer physically present, he tells his disciples, then those who really loved him should go on to love others—*lots* of others—just as they had loved him. "Inasmuch as ye have done it unto one of the least of these, my brethren, ye have done it to me." If you can't, in fact, go on to love others, you never truly loved him to begin with.

But you don't need to take it from Christ. Maude in the movie *Harold and Maude* says the same thing: Love more. Start with your siblings, or your spouse, or your parents, but don't stop there. Love whoever needs what you have; love the ones who have been placed in your path.

It seems so obvious, doesn't it? It is the kind of knowledge we all should know, and instead even the wisest need reminders. Fortunately, the reminders do come, from sages and prophets and out of the mouths of babes: If your heart breaks, *let it break open*. Love more.

Chapter Seventeen

Oh, I *love* that guy!" my Finnish friend, Kalla, shrieked when I admitted to her that I was dating Simon. I don't usually think of Scandinavians as excitable people, but Kalla was actually jumping up and down as she enumerated Simon's various virtues; his courtesy, his gifts as artist and teacher, and what Kalla referred to as his "seeks pax."

"I've seen him working out at the Y," Kalla confessed. "A wonderful person for sure, but he also has a *great body!*"

"He does?" I said.

"You haven't noticed?"

"It's winter in Maine," I excused myself. "Layers of woolen clothing obscure these details." But then, Simon later told me, he had actually shaved off his beard between our first date and our second; I never noticed the difference. *I'd make a horrible witness,* I thought. *But I'd make an excellent nun!*

It helped, anyway, that my friends already knew and liked Simon. In fact, everyone in the community seemed to know him, and he was held in high esteem. That's one good thing about dating a middle-aged man: He has a track record. If the best predictor of future behavior is past behavior, a twenty-year-old doesn't have a lot of past to go by. Drew and I married on instinct or pure dumb luck. Simon could be Googled.

I wasn't supposed to be Googling Simon, however. I was supposed to be writing a sermon on spiritual experience. Seated in my office, before the lighted rectangle of my computer screen, I burst into song:

"And He walks with me and He talks with me
And He tells me I am His own
And the joy we share as we tarry there
Is like nothing I've ever known."

And my children snickered.

"Children!" I said. "It's a hymn!"

"Yeah, right," said Zach.

He doubtless suspected me of dating, though I hadn't told the kids about Simon. The wounds inflicted by the end of my relationship with the ex-boyfriend we now occasionally referred to as He Who Must Not Be Named were still fresh, and I wanted to spare them hope and therefore disappointment.

"It is a religious song," I insisted. "It's from a Baptist hymnal." To which Zach said, Sure, Mom. Whatever.

How shall one describe an intensity of religious experience without drifting into language that can, when taken out of context, seem more suited to romance than liturgy? How could St. Teresa of Avila or an American Pentecostal physically enact the powerful tumult in her God-shaken soul without the spasms, tremblings, moans, and cries more ordinarily ascribed to orgasm? Still, ecstasy is not the constant in either sexuality or religion, though a little ecstasy now and then keeps things perking nicely along.

Don't think about ecstasy, I told myself firmly. And wondered: *What might Google tell Simon about me?*

If you had asked me at twenty to list my really significant flaws, I probably would have said something like "One of my breasts is larger than the other." I seriously imagined that a man worth marrying might consider this a deal-breaker. (Obviously, Drew didn't.)

Fast forward to 2004: A cumulative total of eight years of breastfeeding had mysteriously evened out my breasts, which now dangled in comfy symmetry on either side of my navel. No matter; physical imperfections were not topmost in my mind when fretting about what Simon might regard as problematic about me. Fortunately and unfortunately, I knew what the real deal-breakers could be.

"Full disclosure," I announced to Simon. "I don't notice things."

"No kidding," said Simon, and told me about his beard.

"Well, and I eat snow. And I'm terrible with money."

"That's okay," said Simon. "We live in Maine. No money, plenty of snow."

"And I tend to be a bit haphazard about changing the oil

in the car, or cleaning the lint trap on the dryer. My mother says I'm good on creation, not so good on maintenance."

"Uh-huh," said Simon. He didn't seem too worried yet.

Taking a deep breath, I said, "Put out your hand." He did, and I deposited a small, smooth blob of silvery metal in his palm.

"Wow! Thank you," he said. He turned the blob over in his fingers admiringly. "What is it?"

"It's my teakettle."

Did I intend to make my teakettle into an interesting little art object? No. I'd *intended* to boil water for coffee. Then I wandered off, got involved in some project or other. Hours later, as I happened by the kitchen, I noticed a strange smell. The stove top was covered with blobs of bubbling, silvery goo. By some miracle, I stopped myself from poking at the goo with my index finger, and the molten aluminum, or zinc, or whatever it was eventually cooled. I chiseled it off the enameled surface of the stove and offered a representative sample to Simon. "You need to know this," I said. "I am the kind of person who absentmindedly smelts pots."

"Pot*s*?" said Simon. "How many teakettles have you…?"

"Five," I said.

It was spring. The world was loud with it: Newly awakened creatures squeaked and scurried, intent on the urgent missions of the season. A sweet wind blew, lifting winter's detritus and sending bundles and clumps of twigs and old leaves skittering across the roadways.

"It's hard to tell the creatures from the leaves," I told Monica. "I need a bumper sticker that says I BREAK FOR WINDBLOWN DEBRIS."

Driving down my driveway one morning, I nearly ran over two little chickadees locked in mortal combat. Each was intent on poking out his opponent's beady little eye, or yanking out a few wing feathers. Neither noticed the thousand-pound vehicle rolling and honking in their direction, or the bipedal primate laughing at them from behind the wheel. One finally extricated himself from his enemy's claws and beat a strategic retreat toward the apple trees, with the other in hot pursuit, no doubt shrieking insults about chickadee impotence and cowardice.

"How did you know they were male?" Jeremy asked when I told him this story.

"Duh," said Melanie. Then she laughed, and kissed him.

Knitting, and idly eavesdropping while I waited for a Maine Criminal Justice Academy graduation ceremony to begin, I overheard the following conversation:

"Did you hear I got myself a new husband?" A woman seated in front of me said to the woman beside her.

"Oh, Lord, what did you do that for?" her friend answered disgustedly. "Why didn't you just get a dog? Dogs take less time to die."

They laughed.

Several friends (women) to whom I told this story laughed.

I like to think I am a reasonably good-humored person, but I didn't laugh at this joke. As a police officer's widow, I guess I am poorly positioned to find humor in remarks about dead husbands, and anyway, I was feeling pretty tender and protective of the breastless and betesticled that day. I had just spent a few weeks in northern Maine with game wardens, nearly all of whom are male.

The Maine Warden Service dive team was getting ready to deploy (yet another snowmobile under the ice: it was an early spring epidemic of these), and the wardens who would provide logistical support for the divers were huddled together making plans. The wind was blowing so hard that if I raised my arms, I'd sail. This would have been more fun if the wind hadn't seemed so determined to blow me toward the water. The water had a hard, unnerving gleam, black as obsidian, beyond the white edge of the ice.

Today's dive would be dangerous. The equipment could freeze, the severe cold would enervate the divers' bodies, and true warmth and shelter were a long snowmobile ride away. I don't think body size is a primary qualification for membership on the dive team—the one woman on the team, Irene, is smaller than I am—but the team boasts a lot of large men, tall, broad, apparently invincible. Still, the wind was so black and cold, thick with ice crystals. The ice would be a thick, hard shell above the divers' heads. Though I could catch only parts of sentences that were blown away as soon as they were spoken, I knew the wardens were discussing the procedures they would carry out should one of the divers get into trouble in the water. I can pray and fret, but Glenn knows how to get the airboat moving swiftly to the rescue, and Andy is a qualified paramedic, and they are all strong, determined, and loving. It would be all right.

I raised my arms and sailed a little. The sun poured light over the wide, white expanse of frozen lake, over the mountains beyond, and over these men. Light-washed, they were breathtakingly beautiful. On the verge of tears, I had to look away.

A game warden pulls over an old feller on a snowmobile on a trail up around Moosehead Lake. The game warden comes up to the old feller and says, "Sir, were you aware that your wife fell off the back of your snowmobile about five miles back along the trail?" Old feller says "Oh, thank God! I thought I was going deaf."

In my line of work, it helps to have a sense of humor.

"What qualifications should a law enforcement chaplain have?" I was asked during a presentation I gave on the Maine Warden Service chaplaincy. (My audience was primarily fellow clergy.)

"Well, to begin with, you have to like men," I answered.

I didn't mean one would have to be heterosexual if female or homosexual if male. Rather, law enforcement remains a predominantly male endeavor in both its demographics and its prevailing ethos; most police officers are men, and law enforcement agencies are by and large patterned after traditionally masculine military models. Police officers use traditionally male tools (muscles, guns) to perform a traditionally male service, that of protecting the relatively less powerful.

There are plenty of people who prefer working in a predominantly female environment. "Nothing wrong with that," either, I assured them. "My, um, friend Simon…" (Could I call him a friend? We'd only been out on one date.) "He, um…functions just beautifully in the mostly female world of secondary education, if the enthusiasm of his students and colleagues is anything to go by. He enjoys being around women and is comfortable in groups designed to make decisions by consensus. He doesn't object to allowing everyone's views and feelings to be aired, and he likes tea.

"Personally," I admitted, "I like coffee and a chain of command."

I love men. God help me, I do.

And I don't mean, I love men because men are human beings *mas o menos* and I am a general lover of humanity, so men are okay *mas o menos*. I am not saying that I love everything about men except that they are men.

I mean I love men. Why? Well, here's a partial list off the top of my head (and I should apologize ahead of time, because it is loaded with stereotypes and clichés): I love the way men know how to repair things. I love the way they don't necessarily talk about everything they feel. I love that they know how to set up and work within hierarchies. Hierarchies are very useful sometimes.

I love men's bodies, of course, and I both fear and love the willingness men have to put their bodies in the way of danger, informally as companions, or more deliberately as law enforcement officers, firefighters, and soldiers. I love them for defending not only their own children but mine too.

I love the energy in young men, the passion and fire, and I love the way that same fire smolders, banked in the hearts of the ancient-of-days. I love men's strength, and I love them in those moments when their strength has failed and their bewilderment shows.

"For thousands of years, women have had responsibility without power—while men have had power without responsibility." This is a quote from *The Declaration of the Women's Global Strategies Meeting*. It was written by my old feminist heroine Robin Morgan, and I found it pinned up on the bulletin board of my Unitarian Universalist church in Rockland, Maine.

For thousands of years, women have had responsibility without power—while men have had power without responsibility.

Power without responsibility? I'd love to hear Robin Morgan try to say that line out loud while standing in the middle of Arlington National Cemetery. Or in a coal mine in Appalachia. Or beside Ground Zero in New York.

Who is fit to hold power, the psalmist asks.
And who is worthy to act in God's place?
Those with a passion for the truth

Who are horrified by injustice
Who act with mercy to the poor, and take up the cause of the
  helpless.

Not long ago, I spent the day with wardens whose job it was
to comb a thousand square yards of hilly woodland, locat-
ing the remains of a pilot and his fourteen-year-old daughter.
The small plane had taken off in a late-spring snowstorm the
night before, and hadn't been airborne more than a few minutes before the pilot radioed that he was in trouble.

The bodies were in pieces, half buried in melting snow.
One game warden found part of a small hand. Another found
skin hanging from a thornbush. The pieces were difficult to
locate, but eventually the medical examiner was satisfied that
most of the "cadaver material" had been recovered. They were
carried down out of the woods in large tote bags filled with
smaller zip-lock bags, individually packaged and labeled.

This seems to me a task performed out of extraordinary
kindness, although the wardens don't describe it, or themselves, that way. "Numb" is a more common adjective. "Just
getting the job done" is another phrase that recurs. It snowed
when it shouldn't have, the pilot erred, the plane crashed. "Just
please don't tell me the kid's name," one warden requested.

Their strength is in their compassion
God's light shines through their hearts
Their children's children will bless them
And the work of their hands will endure.

That gas station owner in Rockland, the one who flies and fears falling, and hopes that if the time comes he will remember to do a few backflips as he tumbles from the sky? Next time I see him, I will add a new ending to our shared fantasy: Someone will come to the crash site, gather what is left, bundle us up, and take us home. May whoever that is be blessed. May God defend the goodness in his heart. May God defend the sweetness in his soul.

CHAPTER EIGHTEEN

W hat about the kissing part?" Melanie asked. We had already inked in the processional and recessional music, a nice set of traditional vows, and a prayer or two.

"Then I say 'by the power vested in me by the State of Maine...' blah blah."

"And then we kiss?"

"Well," I said, "there are issues with the kiss."

"Issues?"

"You might as well be aware of them," I said. "You see, back in the day, the minister—that would be me—would, by pronouncing you married, be giving you permission to have sex."

Both of them promptly burst out laughing, and Jeremy blushed scarlet.

"Jeremy would flip back your veil, symbolically undress-ing you, Melanie, and the kiss would be seen as the beginning of your sexual and, not incidentally, your reproductive relationship. Now, my dear children, I don't like to presume about these things, but given that you have already built a house together and are dwelling therein, and given that this is the twenty-first century... let's just say virginity and the taking thereof doesn't seem to be something this ceremony really needs to address.

"However," I said, holding up a hand to quell the giggles and blushes, "I do like to include the kiss in a wedding. Even if you have been having sexual relations with each other before your wedding night, once the vows have been made and the pronouncement pronounced, the wild thing is inextricably part of your marriage. This is true no matter what your erotic behaviors consist of. It can be under-the-kitchen-table night, or dress-up-in-the-bunny-suit night, or sorry-sleepy-quickie night. No matter what it is, married sex affirms the commitment, affirms love, and, of course, if it pleases both of you and God, sex offers the possibility of babies. So if you want the kissing part, we shall have the kissing part."

"I want the kissing part!" Melanie said raptly, while Jeremy muttered, "whydja have to tell her about the bunny suit?"

Woolie's teacher, a pretty young woman in Birkenstock sandals and hand-knit socks, looked pointedly at her watch. I had been late arriving, and the carpool had been waiting for half an hour.

I tumbled out of the car, apologizing breathlessly. "I'm so sorry, Miss Agnew...A child...all-terrain vehicle..." I was still dressed in my warden service uniform, clerical collar still in place. The radio in my truck squawked.

"Oh my goodness," the teacher said, her face filling with understanding and concern. "Was it...very bad?"

I shrugged. "The victim survived."

"Wow," she breathed, shaking her head. "Woolie, what a difficult and important job your mother has, doesn't she?"

Woolie was loading her cello into the back of the truck, and didn't answer. She didn't say much, in fact, until we'd deposited the last of the carpool kids into the arms of their patient parents. "When it was Gordon's birthday, Gordon's mother made the class a homemade organic carrot cake. An *organic* carrot cake," she repeated.

"Yum," I said.

"Sophia's mother comes in every week to help us with our embroidery projects."

"Huh." I was remembering the little girl lying on her side on the hospital gurney, her hands folded across her chest.

"Daphne's dad makes her lunch every morning," Woolie went on peevishly. "He packs a hand-woven wicker basket with brie and baguette, and carob soy milk in a little box with a built-in straw, and fresh figs."

Fresh figs!?

"Look, I'm a widowed mother of four," I had told Woolie's teacher on the first day of school. "I work as a law enforcement chaplain, and I'm on call statewide, twenty-four/seven for dire emergencies." My strong implication was that I would have to be cut some slack, participation-wise.

On the day of the class party, I contributed a box of powdered crullers from the convenience store. Woolie makes her own lunch (figless). I even managed to avoid being a chaperone on any of the character-building class camping trips that Woolie always described, with proud exhaustion, as being akin to the Bataan Death March.

Still, on this very afternoon, in the autumn of her eighth grade year, Woolie asked if I would please be the class parent for the following month.

Maybe I recalled the image of another mother, the one who had to be yanked resentfully from an alcohol-enhanced oblivion and driven to the hospital because the all-terrain babysitter nearly killed her child. I said yes.

"It would be great!" Miss Agnew enthused the next day. She is a fresh-faced young woman with an intimidating air of vigorous competence. "As a mother of four, you will bring so much relevant experience to our next unit study!"

"I will?"

"Sure! Didn't Woolie tell you? Our next unit study is about human sexuality and reproduction."

Oh.

"Woolie didn't tell me. How delightful. But I don't know if really am the *best* parent to help with this particular unit study," I said. "You see, my children were all accidents."

"Oh! Oh, dear."

"Well," I amended. "Not all of them. Peter was planned. But the rest were the results of ghastly errors."

"I see."

"For a while there, I was like some kind of queen termite. The larvae just kept squirting out, one after another—"

"Perhaps," Miss Agnew interrupted hastily, "it would be better if I covered the functional, *practical* aspects of our topic. And you could do...I know! You can do the *values* piece."

"Values?"

"Sure! Morality, meaningful relationships, and so forth. Since..." Miss Agnew, obviously having received further inspiration, went on delightly: "Since you're a woman of the cloth!"

Oh. That. "All right," I said reluctantly. "But I'm not baking anything."

"Someone else will handle the snacks," Miss Agnew assured me.

It could still fall through, I warned her hopefully. Hurricane Katrina had recently devastated the Gulf Coast, and technically I was on call to go to New Orleans. As the days leading up to the start of the human sexuality and reproduction unit study flew relentlessly by, I nurtured secret hopes that an urgent call from FEMA would extract me from having to teach sexual values to thirteen-year-olds. FEMA's legendary inefficiency precluded an honorable and timely deployment, however, and so at last the day came. There I was, standing before a dozen snickering adolescents next to a blackboard on which someone had thoughtfully written the word *SEX*.

I scowled at the word, and then at the children.

"Children!" I said. "I am Reverend Braestrup. As Woolie will no doubt affirm, I am a stiff and puritanical person. So we're not, I repeat, *not* going to talk about sex."

"Ohhhhhh…" they groaned, disappointed (all except Woolie, whose pink face registered profound relief).

"Well," I amended, "we *are* going to have to talk about sex, but only a tiny bit. As the official parent assistant for this unit study, I suppose I do have to make sure you know where babies come from." I glared at them suspiciously. "Do you know where babies come from?"

The students guffawed and poked at each other, kicked at invisible debris beneath their desks, and finally admitted that yes, they knew where babies come from.

"Will someone please fill me in?"

Silence.

"Come on. Enlighten me." Silence. Ah, and my eye fell on Gordon, the boy whose mother makes *organic carrot cake*. "I'll bet you can tell me, can't you, Gordon?"

"Um," squeaked Gordon. "Well…the man and the woman lie down, and, um…"

"I can't hear him," said Crystal.

"A teensy bit louder, Gordon dear."

"The man, um, the man…the man does…Well, he puts…"

It took a while, but I finally got Gordon to admit that the

man inserts his penis into the woman's vagina. There was an explosion of giggling, hooting, elbowing, kicking, eye-rolling, and hissed accusations of terminal immaturity. "Okay now!" I proclaimed above the din: "Let's all say it together: THE MAN PUTS HIS PENIS IN THE WOMAN'S VAGINA!"

We chanted it a few times, at first hesitantly, then with increasing confidence. We began to vary the emphases; we made it into reggae with a little rhythmic drumming on the desktops: "THE MAN PUTS HIS PENIS IN THE WOMAN'S VAGINA...THE MAN PUTS HIS PENIS IN THE WOMAN'S VAGINA..." When the decibel level was sufficient to rattle the jars of naturally pigmented liquid watercolors on the art supplies shelf, I brought it to an end with a fierce look and declared them all adequately sex-educated for the purposes of the day's discussion. I erased the word *SEX* from the board. In its place I scrawled, in shaky capitals:

NOTHING MATTERS MORE THAN _____.

Silence.

"Sex?" squeaked Gordon.

"No!" I said. "No more sex! We're moving on to the *values* part now." I tapped the chalk impatiently under the blank space: "Come on, kids. What matters to you?"

"Painting pictures," said Woolie.

"Doing well at school," said Jane.

"My parents," said Gordon.

"Well, of course there's my horse, Toby," Daphne mused. She sighed dreamily. "I love my horse Toby."

"Daphne, we all, like, *know* you have a horse. You don't have to keep bragging," said Crystal.

"I am not bragging," cried Daphne. "Toby matters, like, so much!"

"Hip-hop!" shouted Fred.

"Snowboarding!" shrieked Sophia.

Gordon raised his hand. "The earth," he said quietly.

Family, beauty, art, music… "Life!" said Olive suddenly, as if struck by the obvious.

I had been madly scribbling, trying to get all their suggestions on the blackboard. "The earth, friendship, pets… these are definitely things that matter. Which one matters *most*?"

There was a long silence. "This is actually, like, hard," said Crystal, rubbing the bridge of her nose where her little round glasses pinched.

"Isn't it?" I said. "I think so too, Crystal. It's surprisingly hard."

"Will there be a test?" asked Jane.

"No, sweet-pea. No test, at least not in school. And I'll tell you something else: You will probably spend the rest of your life not only answering this question, but also figuring out how to live your life according to what your answer turns out to be. Once you've filled in the blank, this sentence will become, in effect, your working definition of God."

"*Wow*," the children said, and gazed at the chalkboard with greater intensity.

"Now, I told Miss Agnew and your parents that I couldn't really talk to you about morals and values when it comes to sex until I let you know the basis for what I had to say about those things. In other words, I have to fill in the blank on the blackboard."

"You're going to give us the answer?" asked Jane hopefully, her pencil poised.

"I'm not giving you the answer. I'm giving you my answer. Your answer might be different, and your parents' answer might be different too."

I turned and marked four letters firmly in chalk, and Daphne read the result out loud. "Love."

"Love?" said Fred disappointedly.

"*That's* your working definition of God?" asked Daphne. She sounded disappointed too.

"Simple, isn't it?"

"Schmaltzy," said Sophia.

"I love mustard," Fred admitted.

"Yeah, well, you're weird," said someone, to which Fred responded with some inappropriate physical contact; mild profanity was heard, and insults exchanged. Once we'd moved beyond this episode, I admitted that I loved knitting, eating crushed ice, and picking apples.

"Other languages have many words for all the various emotions and intentions we call love," I went on. "And if we weren't so lazy, Americans would say 'I am awfully fond of mustard,' or 'I have a great affinity for hip-hop music.'

Instead, we end up saying 'I love ice cubes' and 'I love justice,' and 'Oooh, I just *love* Leonardo DiCaprio!' all with the same word.

"So if I'm going to talk about the kind of love that matters most, I'm going to have to teach you a little Greek. Don't groan! You can learn three Greek words in the service of your sex education; it's not too much to ask.

"In Jesus' day, people within the confines of the Roman Empire might speak several languages, but the one they all had in common was *koine* Greek. Jesus himself probably spoke Aramaic, but because he was a carpenter, and carpenters have to be able to conduct business..."

"My dad is a carpenter," said Daphne. "He built a special little barn for my horse Toby."

"Jesus would have been able to speak enough Greek to buy nails, or to negotiate contracts with people who wanted him to build a special little barn for their horses. So Jesus would have known at least three words in Greek to use when he talked to his disciples about love.

"And—brace yourselves—the first word is fortuitously applicable to our unit study! It is the word *eros.*" I wrote it on the board in English and then, just to show off, in Greek. "Who can guess what *eros* means?"

"Erotic?" guessed Gordon.

"Brilliant, Gordon! And when something is erotic, it's...?"

"Sexy," said Fred, wriggling his skinny body in his seat.

"Exactly! *Eros* refers to romantic and sexual love, to desire, passion, the kind of feelings that lovers have for each other. But it can also be used to describe the feeling a gourmet has for good food, or an art collector has for beautiful objects. There's nothing wrong with *eros,* incidentally. You don't have to reject it; in fact, you can and will enjoy it. Still, in the long run, *eros* doesn't satisfy. And you should know that *eros* is the love that is most prone to corruption. It's the one that most easily turns into something other than love…"

"Like into hate?" said Fred. "My big brother hates his girlfriend. She done him wrong."

"That happens," I said, nodding sympathetically. "In addition, eros can lead us to treat other people as objects or a means to our own ends instead of as human beings who are as real and important as we are."

"It's like his girlfriend didn't think about his feelings at all—she just went ahead and done him wrong."

"And think about someone who goes out with a boy because she knows he'll buy her the perfume she wants, or a boy who wishes he had a girlfriend the way he wishes for a motorcycle, or a particular brand of sneakers: because it will make his friends think he's cool. Love that treats a person as a source of stuff, or as a possession, isn't really love at all."

"*Eros* is bad," said Fred. "Ask my brother."

"It isn't bad," I insisted. "Where would art or music be without *eros,* where would science be without the pleasure and passion that we feel when we discover something new about the world? Eros is a good thing, but it is strong and it's tricky, and it is easy to make mistakes with it."

"My brother's woman made a big mistake," said Fred darkly.

"The next kind of love is *philos*," I went on briskly, and wrote it on the board in two languages. Jane carefully copied my Greek. "*Philos* is usually translated as 'brotherly love.' It is affection, friendship, good-natured love. In general, *philos* isn't associated with strong passion, but it is durable and relatively incorruptible.

"Remember when I said that once you fill in the blank this sentence is your functional definition of God? In the Bible, in the Gospel of John, there is a very short verse that says '*God is love*.' The word *love* used there is not *eros* or *philos*. It is this word: *agape*. This is also the word for *love* that St. Paul uses in his letter to the Corinthians: *Agape* is patient, *agape* is kind, *agape* is not envious or boastful or rude."

"Yeah, *Daphne*," said Crystal pointedly.

"Shut up."

"*Agape* is not irritable or resentful…"

"Ha-*ha*, Crystal."

"Ahem!" I aimed a glare at them. "*Agape* does not rejoice in wrongdoing, but rejoices in the truth. It bears all things, believes all things, hopes all things, endures all things…"

"That's a lot," said Gordon thoughtfully.

"It is a lot. *Agape*, incidentally, became the Latin word *caritas*, from which we get our word *charity*. Agape, or *caritas*, is unconditional, selfless, and self-giving. It is love that is offered entirely for the well-being of the beloved, a love that earnestly desires the wholeness and happiness of the one who is loved."

"It's how parents love," said Daphne.

"It's how parents *at their best* love," I said carefully, thinking of the drunken mother, the deadbeat dad, my own hand striking Peter's bum. "Which is why God is so often referred to in the Bible as a parent. Jesus even calls God *Abba*, which means 'Daddy.' It's as if the biblical writers couldn't imagine anything more powerful, reliable, and wonderful than a parent's love. Still, even a good parent will sometimes forget how to love, and will treat a child as a source of satisfaction or a burden, and not as a human being."

"Yeah, *Mom*," said Woolie sharply from the back row.

"And children can forget at least as easily that their parents are likewise human," I said. "Well, what can you expect? We're not Gods, so we're bound to err. Still, if the language in the Bible is anything to go by (and sometimes it is, my children), the kind of love we are called to offer to God and neighbor, to receptionists and classmates, husbands and children, to those we feel *eros* or feel *philos* for, and even to our enemies, is this." I tapped my chalk against the word. "When Jesus says to love your enemies, *agape* is the word he uses."

"I don't love my enemies," said Sophia firmly. "I don't even like them."

"If he uses this word, though, maybe he's saying we don't

have to *like* our enemies," said Olive thoughtfully. "If we were supposed to like them, he would have used *philos*."

"Or *eros*, if we were supposed to feel, you know, sexy about our enemies," Gordon put in.

"That would be *sick*, dude," said Fred.

"But we have to want them to be happy," said Olive.

"Because Jesus said so? You know, Wooliesmother, my family is Muslim," said Fred. "I don't have to listen to Jesus."

"All of us are free to listen or not listen to anyone we like, darling boy, as long as we're generally polite about it. But Muslims do see Jesus as a prophet, a wise man, and by the way, Mahayana Buddhists view him as a bodhisattva, a compassionate teacher of enlightenment. Jesus was teaching us about the kind of love that can make the world a better place and help each of us to be a happier and better person. That might be good information to have."

"It just sounds so hard," said Olive. "Especially the part about loving your enemies."

"I know," I said sympathetically. "It's hard enough to love your friends! And we are supposed to try to love this way not just when we are at church, or praying, or actually thinking about God. It's how we should try to be all the time, in all situations."

"Even sex?" said Fred, drumming a reggae rhythm on his desk with his pencil. (He was obviously hoping we could start the penis-and-vagina reggae chant again.)

"Oh yes, Fred. Even sex," I said indulgently. "*Especially* sex."

Their homework was to ask their parents to "fill in the blank."

"Are we going to talk more about sex tomorrow?" Crystal asked as we finished our dessert. Gordon's mother had provided organic vegan cupcakes, which were unbelievably delicious. (I was actually beginning to really like Gordon's mother.)

"Tomorrow, children," I said, licking organic vegan icing from my thumb, "we shall read the Bible." They groaned, of course.

Chapter Nineteen

Once upon a time, there was a nice lady, an ordained minister, a woman of the cloth, who went to the YMCA. She and her lovely children planned to go swimming in the pool.

Now, at this particular YMCA, members were given membership cards with a magnetic strip that you were supposed to swipe on your way in. That way, the YMCA would know who was in the building.

Our woman of the cloth hardly ever had to swipe her card, however, because the people behind the desk knew her and her family. So they would walk by, and the people behind the desk would wave, and it was all very pleasant and easy.

Well, on this occasion, the woman behind the desk stopped the ordained mother minister and said, "We have a new policy. We aren't allowed to let anyone in without swiping."

Well. The minister had five of those cards altogether, one for her and for each of her four lovely children, and they were buried at the bottom of one of the swim bags. She didn't even know which bag. And it had already been a long day.

"Do I really have to?" the minister said, and the woman behind the counter said yes. So the poor, overworked ordained minister mother had to pull out all the towels and swimsuits out of all the bags, and she sighed a lot while she was doing this, rather loudly, and rolled her eyes. When she finally found the cards—in the bottom of the very last bag, of course—she swiped them through the little machine sharply, angrily, like so, and stomped off to the dressing room. She was just wriggling into her bathing suit *when she remembered.*

A pause for dramatic effect. I was telling this story to Woolie's sex education class.

"What did you remember?" asked Gordon.

Ruefully, I tapped the blackboard. *"Nothing matters more than love."*

"Ahhh," the children chorused.

"So I had to take off my swimsuit, put my clothes back on. I had to go all the way back upstairs to the reception desk, where I told the woman I was sorry for being so crabby and unkind."

"Did she forgive you?" asked Olive.

"She did, in fact. She is a nice lady. I still feel bad about it. I mean, this was a pretty easy test of my ability to love, and I flunked it."

"You're only human," said Gordon sympathetically.

*   *   *

Maybe Simon sometimes fails at love? I know he has quirks. He regularly misplaces his wallet and is nearly always late for appointments. He can't go anywhere without meeting someone he knows, and can't resist engaging in conversation when such meetings occur. (Thus, he is nearly always late for appointments.)

Perhaps he'll change? Perhaps we both will: I expected, even assumed, that improvement was possible when I was young, and okay, I am more alert than I used to be, and Simon has so disciplined himself that he is seldom more than five or ten minutes late, he says. Still, we have been recognizably ourselves for decades and can expect to be exactly who we are for all the decades still to come. At least as middle-aged people we know and can name our intransigent faults, the ones that will not change, the ones that must therefore be confessed to and forgiven if love is to last.

"I've never been much of a sunbather," I confided to Lieutenant Allen, who was giving me a lift to Augusta. On the sunnier side of his house, he had told me, crocuses pushed their determined way through a crust of dirty snow. On the muddy front lawn of a house in Union, we saw an equally determined young woman lying on a folding lawn chaise in a bathing suit, eagerly and obstinately soaking up the sun.

"I don't tan. But," I said, and snorted irritably, "Simon tans."

The lieutenant raised his eyebrows in tolerant inquiry. "You mean he likes to lie around on the beach?"

"No. I mean that when he's out in the sun for any amount of time, Simon's skin turns this extraordinary golden-brown color. I've never seen anything like it."

"Really." The lieutenant drove with his right hand. He had his left elbow parked on the truck's window ledge, and his index finger draped across his upper lip. He looked suspiciously as if he was smiling.

"His children do it too. I mean, there's Ilona, his daughter, with her blue eyes and long red hair. You put that kid on a beach for an hour and she bronzes. *Bronzes!* Meanwhile, my children and I will be huddled resentfully on our beach towels, coated with SPF four thousand, and turning—at best—a slightly grubbier shade of mottled pink."

Back in the bad old days, before SPF, I would slather myself in baby oil and lie out in the sun, trying hard to change color. Bright and painful red turned out to be the only available option. Having chosen this once too often, and also having lived in the tropics as a child, I'm pretty much guaranteed to lose parts of my face to basal cell carcinoma.

"I've got the genes. Grandparents on both sides had skin cancer. It's sort of a family tradition, to have your nose whittled away, bit by cancerous bit, starting from about sixty-five. So anyway, I'm thinking this relationship may not work out in the long run," I told Lieutenant Allen.

"How do you figure?" he asked, startled.

"There I'll be, with my pale flab, no nose, and big cancerous growths all over my face, and Simon will look like an ad for Ban de Soleil."

"Cheez, Katie! Give the guy a break! You'd think being good-looking was a bad thing."

"Well, not in some people, El-Tee," I said, smiling at him. "I mean, it doesn't bother me that *you're* a hottie."

"Good to know," said the lieutenant comfortably.

"He's just so wretchedly wonderful. It's disconcerting," I confessed.

"I dunno. I thought that idea you had about joining a convent was disconcerting. I like ol' Simon. Nice feller," said the lieutenant judiciously. He had met Simon at another warden's retirement party not long before. "And he's got a nice bod."

I sighed gloomily.

"It's not a bad thing, Katie." The lieutenant chuckled. "It's really okay to be happy. You'll get used to it."

The game warden Jesse Gillespie majored in wildlife biology at Unity College. He knows a lot about animals and natural history. He has a deep affection for that ordinary example of American wildlife, the raccoon. "They can live wherever and they'll eat whatever," he said admiringly. "Completely adaptable. I raised an orphaned raccoon when I was a kid. I named him Rascal, after the one in the book. He had these great little black paws, like soft little hands."

"Did you give him a sugar cube and watch him try to wash it?" I asked. "Like in the book?"

"Oh, yeah. Mean trick," said Jesse, laughing.

"My dogs treed a whole family of raccoons in our back-yard in Thomaston last week," I said. "They were so pleased with themselves."

"You have hounds?"

"Not exactly." Actually, our canine contingent consisted of our now adolescent Jack Russell terrier, Chaos, and our ancient, blind retriever-collie mix, Lassie. Between them, Chaos and Lassie had managed to send the mother raccoon and her four little babies up the slanting trunk of a maple tree. I heard the hullabaloo from the kitchen and went out to see.

Chaos was beside himself with excitement. He strutted about on his bandy little legs, squeaking and yipping in what he clearly believed was a plausible imitation of his ferocious lupine ancestors. Blind old Lassie was doing her best to help, barking toothlessly, but with spirit, in the general direction of the compost bin.

The mother raccoon ushered her children to the crotch of a convenient branch, then settled herself, gazing disdain-fully down at this noisy, hapless remnant of a wolf pack.

"They are so cute!" said Woolie of the baby raccoons, and they really were, gazing wide-eyed through their little bandit masks from behind the safe bulwark of their mother's body.

On seeing us, Chaos barked even more hysterically, and peed triumphantly on the base of the maple. The effect of this territorial display was somewhat spoiled by Chaos's tendency, though he had recently learned to lift his leg, to piddle mostly on his own sternum.

The mother raccoon was easily twice the size of Chaos, and more experienced. She could have marched down that tree trunk and kicked his tiresome puppy ass. But four baby raccoons clung to their mother's fat, furry body, and she couldn't leave them behind. So the mother sighed heavily and lodged herself comfortably against the bark, prepared to wait out the siege.

We didn't make her wait long; I called the dogs into the house—Chaos panting proudly, wagging his stumpy tail, Lassie stumbling eagerly toward her food dish, banging into the leg of the kitchen table en route.

As soon as these irritants had been removed, the mother raccoon disentangled herself and her babies from the branches and led a leisurely parade down the tree trunk. She squeezed easily through the wire fence and disappeared into my neighbor's shrubbery. The babies tumbled along behind her, their pajama-striped tails erect, obedient and orderly save for the last and smallest baby, who squawked, wanted to be carried, nipped provocatively at her nearest sibling's rump, and generally behaved quite a lot like someone I could mention. (I did mention it, in fact, and Woolie was appropriately miffed.)

Later, sitting on the couch with the children and reading aloud one of the scarier parts of *Harry Potter,* I remembered the mother raccoon and felt my kinship with her so strongly that I could almost imagine that the young bodies pressed in around me had fur.

"Raccoons are as common as dirt," Jesse was saying as we drove along through the fresh fall afternoon. "It always makes me sad to see 'em lying by the side of the road. More so than porcupines, which is illogical. But I remember the way Rascal used to hold on to my finger with his little black paws. Their paws are wicked soft." He paused, reminiscing. The truck went around a bend in the road, and as if on cue, there was a dead raccoon resting amid the weeds as if in slumber, its front paws folded tidily across its chest.

"I wonder," Jesse said, after a time, "if raccoons are getting smarter."

"You mean, smarter than we are?"

"Nah." Jesse snorted as if he didn't consider that a particularly high standard to exceed. "I mean, what if our vehicle traffic is basically selecting for raccoons who are capable of understanding the threat a car poses to their survival? Or selecting for raccoons who can judge distance and speed?"

"You mean, raccoons could be evolving into brainier animals," I said.

"Yeah!" said Jesse. "Exactly!" He looked around at the passing woods, clearly envisioning a race of super-Procyon doing algebraic equations beneath the birches. Then he shot a sidelong glance at his chaplain, Reverend Braestrup, sitting there in the passenger seat in her uniform and clerical collar. "Do you, um..." he began carefully. "Do you believe in, you know, evolution?"

"No, Jesse," I said. "I don't."

"Oh," he said.

"I don't *believe* in the theory of evolution; I am *convinced by it.*"

"That's semantics," said Jesse, scowling: I'd given him a scare, and he was annoyed with me.

"Sorry. You're right. But the distinction is important, at least to me. If I am convinced by the theory of evolution, it means I could potentially be unconvinced. That's what makes a science a science: Scientific theories, like the heliocentric solar system, or the theory of gravity, can be disproven should new evidence arise."

"It's not too likely," said Jesse, "that evolution would be disproved."

"No, it's not. But it's theoretically possible. What I *believe*, on the other hand, I believe without reference to scientific evidence. What I believe I could not be made to disbelieve."

"So, um," said Jesse, "what do you believe?"

"I believe that *God is love,*" I told him.

"That's it?" said Jesse.

"That's it."

"Oh," said Jesse.

"Pathetically simple. But," I said, and opened my mouth, preparing to pour forth the full lesson. No doubt he would have found it illuminating; perhaps he would have thought me brilliant. But Jesse interrupted:

"You know, I hate to break this to you, Kate. No offense, but I don't believe in love...I am *not convinced by* love anymore," he corrected himself scornfully.

"Is that right?"

"Georgina...my wife. She says she's tired of living on game warden pay, tired of living in the woods. She says she's all done. With me," Jesse said, and pulled over to the side of the road.

Though I may speak in tongues of mortals and of angels, but have not love... Damn. I shut my silly, clanging mouth and let him cry.

Chapter Twenty

When it comes to exploring and explaining what it means to be human, living in the world, we default, perforce, to metaphor. "When my dad died my heart broke."

This isn't true, is it? After all, while the left ventricle wall of the hollow muscular pump situated in the left-center of my father's chest ruptured, his daughter's heart kept right on beating, intact.

Upon being informed of the decease of her father, the subject experienced a severe emotional shock triggering intense emotional and physiological arousal, characterized by elevations in levels of hormones and neurotransmitters including, though not limited to, epinephrine and norepinephrine and the corticosteroids, with resultant elevations in both systolic and diastolic blood pressure, blood sugar, heart rate, and rate of respiration…

I love science. I am fascinated by it, particularly by evolutionary biology, an interest I share with Jesse. More than once

I have been the beneficiary of scientific medicine's wondrous ability when the lives of my children were snatched from the jaws of death. Once, when Ellie was released from the hospital after a particularly nasty bout of pneumonia, I wanted to bring the IV and the oxygen tank to church (and the antibiotics and steroids, the pediatrician and the nurses), place them on the altar, and prostrate myself before them. *Hail, all hail glorious Science! That freed the breath of life and gave my little girl back to me*... But I am not a scientist. I'm not even a theologian. I am a chaplain, a pastor, a maker of metaphors, a teller of tales.

"Jesse," I said gently. "Are any commandments being broken?'

Jesse lifted his blue gaze to the ceiling and stared at it intently. He raised his fist and held it against his mouth, as if to stop himself from saying something his own ears weren't up to hearing. "I don't think I'm breaking any," he said at last.

"You aren't sure about Georgina."

"*Thou shalt not kill,* right?" he said. "Well, I'll tell you, this is killing me. I'm not sleeping."

"No kidding," I said kindly, looking at the ink circles underneath his eyes.

"I know. I look like hell."

"Just tired."

"Food tastes like dust. My uniform pants are getting loose enough that pretty soon I'll be able to take them off without unbuttoning them. And I can't breathe," Jesse said. "That's the weirdest thing. I go to work. I check on fishing holes, look for deer baits, talk to people, and the whole time I'm struggling to take in enough air."

"As if there's a strap fastened around your chest?" I suggested, and he looked at me with that *She's omniscient!* look.

"Exactly like that."

"And how about sex?'

"What? Oh…" he said, turning bright red. "Well, no."

"No sex?"

"Yeah. I mean, it's probably been…I don't know, a month or more since Georgina and I…well, since we were intimate."

"Huh," I said thoughtfully.

"Not that I even care about that right now. I mean, of course I care about it, but I just want Georgina to…I want…"

I really wished the chaplain's office were soundproof. I could hear a secretary chewing gum on the other side of the wall. I could hear the burble and fizz when she opened her Pepsi. Maybe I should play music or one of those CDs of wave sounds so that people can cry in here if they want to.

"Jesse," I said tenderly. "Have you ever thought about becoming a K-9 handler?"

He didn't answer, and after a long silence, I realized that he had cried himself sleep on my office floor. So I covered him with my sweater and let him sleep while I, typing quietly, retrieved my e-mail.

*   *   *

"I think love demands that we take a person seriously, first of all," Simon said. We were sitting in the Bayview Cinema in Camden, waiting for the film to start. (I had already seen it—it was a documentary about paraplegic athletes called *Murderball*, and it's my favorite movie.)

"How do you know so much about love? How did you learn it?" *What is your story, Simon?*

"I don't know that I have really learned it yet," Simon said. "That is, I'm still working on it."

"Well, all right. Sure. But at some point you figured out what it was you wanted to learn. Did you learn it from being married and getting divorced?"

Simon shook his head emphatically. "No." Then he amended this: "Well, actually, yes. I'm sure I learned a lot from that too. But…"

"Yes?"

"You know, I hesitate to say this," he said. "Especially to you. But I learned it at church."

"Really!" I said.

"You sound surprised," he said.

"I am," I answered. "Wow."

Simon was raised Roman Catholic. Unlike my friend Elizabeth, his experiences in church made sense to him: His progressive parish priest (a Jesuit and an antiwar activist) was a family friend and mentor, as well as a guide to what Simon describes as a real relationship with Christ.

"And doing unto others as you would have them do unto

you: I took that very seriously, and thought about it a lot. To love your neighbor as yourself means you have to understand that others are like you, they feel need in the same way. So you give. You give regardless, incidentally, of whether or not they reciprocate."

"Really?" I said, to be quite sure. "And you got this from church?"

"Yes, O Woman of the Cloth. Really."

("He's religious," I would tell Lieutenant Allen the day after this date. "And he can fix *anything*."

"I thought you liked it when guys fixed stuff," Lieutenant Allen protested.

"I like it when guys are religious," I said glumly.

"You're in trouble, Katie," the lieutenant said, chuckling.

"You don't know the half of it," I said. "Get this...")

So there we were at the old Bayview Street Cinema, having a meaningful conversation and waiting to see *Murderball*. The lights went down and the movie began. It clattered loudly through its opening frames, and there was the accompanying smell of burning celluloid. After a few false starts and some audible obscenity from the projection booth, the manager/projectionist appeared. "Sorry, folks," he said. "We are experiencing acute technical difficulties. If you just check in at the popcorn stand, Suzie will refund your money."

The crowd filed politely out to the lobby. Simon, however, approached the manager. "Do you mind if I have a look at the projector?"

"Sure," the manager said. We followed him into the projection booth.

"Um, Simon," I whispered dubiously, "do you know anything about movie projectors?"

Simon shrugged. "No," he admitted. "I'm just interested."

For the next quarter hour, Simon dug around in the entrails of the enormous machine while the manager and Suzie (the popcorn/ticket girl) watched. They entertained Simon with updates on the post-secondary adventures of Suzie's classmates and the manager's son and his classmates, all of whom had been Simon's students at Camden High, while I examined the old movie posters and photographs of starlets that decorated the walls of the projection booth.

Suddenly, the machine gave a sort of metallic burp, flapped a bit of film, and clattered back to life, churning happily in accurate and odor-free projection. There were cries of amazement and gratitude all around. "How did you *do* that?" I demanded in a fierce whisper as we took our seats in the otherwise empty theater, but he just smiled, and enfolded my hand in his.

I did not immediately tell my children I was dating someone. Feeling overwhelmingly responsible for the protection of their psychological health, I delayed their meeting with Simon for as long as possible.

"For one thing," said Simon, as we jointly considered the

timing and conduct of such a first encounter, "there's my name."

Simon's family is American, but both his parents emigrated from Holland and retained the continental pronunciation of their own and their children's names. Thus, Simon was spelled in the expected manner, but he and his family pronounced it "SEE-mun."

"Your name is semen?" my son Zach said in confusion the first time he shook Simon's hand.

"Not semen, sweetheart, *Simon*," I interjected hastily.

"You just said it again," said Zach.

"You did, Mom," his brother agreed. "You said semen."

"Come again?" said Simon, which didn't help.

"The second syllable is *-mon*, as in *Monday*," I explained. "See-munnnn…"

"Mom's dating a guy named Semen!" Peter chortled gleefully. "Wait'll I tell my friends!"

"What is so funny about semen?" Woolie asked, with disingenuous innocence.

"Seee-mun…See-mun," I repeated loudly.

"See-mun," said Ellie dutifully.

"You know, I think the name *Semen* is a little gender exclusive," Zach said thoughtfully. "I'm going to call you Sea-People."

"I'm going to call him the Semenator," Peter shouted from the other room; he was going for the phone.

"I shall call you Simian, because you look a little like a

silverback gorilla," said Ellie, our resident primatologist. "I mean that in a good way," she added politely.

After dinner, Simon and I sat alone together on the couch. "I think this first meeting went pretty well," Simon said. "Your kids didn't seem wary of me."

"Yes," I conceded. "It was good."

"Cobus says you're pretty," Simon told me, putting his arms around me. I'd met his children earlier in the day. It had been a more sedate encounter, but then, I don't have a disconcerting name. (Later, they would derive the usual amusement from calling me "Bra Strap," but not yet.)

"Cobus is a darling boy," I said warmly. Then I sighed.

"Are you sad?"

"Yes. I want so badly to protect my children... They're so sweet, and so vulnerable..." I was weepy. Simon drew me onto his lap and embraced me. Just then, Peter walked in.

"Holy moly!" he shrieked. He turned on his heel. We could hear him racing up the stairs to his siblings' bedrooms: "Hey, Zach, guess what! *Mom has Simon all over her!*"

Chapter Twenty-one

The State of Maine vests me with the power to join two people together in legal matrimony. All the state requires of me is that I elicit two clear, sober, unequivocal statements: "Yes, I want to be married to this woman" and "Yes, I want to be married to this man." Most couples don't want to limit the ceremony to what is merely legal, however, no matter how ambivalent they are about "religious gobbledygook." So we will throw in some other stuff: A younger brother will mumble First Corinthians like an embarrassed robot; a best friend will do a weepy reading of Pablo Neruda, and maybe the bride's wacky Uncle Ronnie will be persuaded to tuck a guitar into his armpit and warble "You Light Up My Life" and everyone will weep.

A person subjects himself to all of this in front of friends and family, and in so doing declares a new, definitive identity. It is a moment of startling vulnerability. *Here,* a man declares, *is my espoused one, the one I choose. Here,* a woman says, *is the parent of my children, the contentment of my years, the companion to my old age.*

As of this writing, a no-fault divorce can take place in Maine within three months of filing. You will have to go to court, however. As a minister, my word can legally inaugurate a marriage, but only a judge can end it.

"If there were to be a ceremony for the end of a marriage, it shouldn't be a milquetoast we'll-always-be-good-friends lie," Warden Jesse Gillespie opined. "It should be honest. The divorcing person should be able to stand up in church, before God and all those beloved witnesses, and say, 'Y'know what? I'll pay my child support every month on time, I will be polite at the kids' graduations and weddings and whatnot, but otherwise I hope and pray and plan to forget that you exist.'"

Jesse was getting divorced. It wasn't his idea. He didn't want to do it, but short of contesting the divorce—which he saw as promising a Pyrrhic victory at best—he would be legally single within mere months. As with most of the divorces initiated in America, his wife was initiating this one, and for the same reason that is given by most divorcing women when they are surveyed. "She says she's bored," Jesse announced.

"Bored?"

"Yeah. I'm boring."

"Oh," I said. My instinct, of course, was to say, *Jesse, I don't find you boring at all.* But my opinion didn't matter . . . or, conversely, it could end up mattering too much. Which is to say that Jesse had already asked if I'd mind going to the movies with him.

I was forced to explain that, tempting though this offer was (and it actually was: I enjoy Jesse's company), it probably wasn't such a good idea.

"I didn't mean it *that* way," Jesse protested hotly, his ears turning crimson.

"Of course you didn't," I agreed. "But other wardens, and particularly other wardens' wives, have to know that I can be trusted to keep the boundaries firm."

"Mike," said Jesse. "He'd think something was up. He's such a puritan."

"Actually, I think he's an American Baptist. Still, because he is such an upstanding Christian, Mike might be the last person to think poorly of others."

"I love that guy. I wish I could be more like Mike. He's so *calm*."

"He is, isn't he? Mike is a treasure."

"He told me once that divorce is forbidden. Because Jesus said so, and what Jesus says tends to go, with Mike."

"Well, he's right," I said. "That is, Jesus did forbid divorce. Jesus even condemned marrying a woman who had been divorced. He said it was adultery."

"Great."

"Now, there are scholars who argue that Jesus' prohibition on divorce had more to do with the harm that was done to women by divorce as it was practiced at the time. But Jesus himself doesn't offer clarification. He just says no divorce, period."

"I could try telling Georgina that Jesus forbids her to ditch me," Jesse said, and he laughed, painfully.

"You could also try asking for more time to work things out."

"She says divorcing is going to make everything better. She says she doesn't want to wait, that she's waited long enough. She says that the only thing I can do now is work at remaining friends." Jesse looked carefully at his hands. "I don't know, Kate. I'll try, I guess, but I don't know if I can stand being friends with Georgina."

It comforted Jesse somewhat to hear that I know of few divorces that end truly amicably, few in which the two parties involved remained friends in any genuine sense of the word.

The best example sat in the third pew most Sundays at the First Universalist Church for more than a decade: Henry, his ex-wife, Julie, and Julie's partner, Danielle.

Henry and Julie were married young and stayed married for a few years, but it never really clicked. Then came a night when they'd each had a few to drink, which made them brave and angry. Julie made a particularly stinging remark about Henry's sex appeal, and Henry responded with "Oh, yeah? Well, I don't like your body either. In fact, I don't even like women!"

There was, Henry would later say, a scary little silence. Then Julie said: "Henry, I think I'm gay too."

So Henry and Julie "remained good friends" because in fact that was all they had ever been. They worked out an impressively amicable divorce. To this day, they support each other financially and emotionally, welcome each other's partners into their lives easily, and sit companionably together most Sundays in the same pew at church.

"I've heard of some heterosexual couples who remain friends too," I assured Jesse. "But they are very few and very far between."

Game wardens who come to me for advice after a divorce frequently express guilt at their failure to be friends with their ex. "Think of how much we have been through with each other!" they'll say. "Besides, we share children—isn't that bond enough to overcome all else?"

"If it were, we'd still be married," said Jesse, and I said, Well, yes. Exactly.

If following a divorce you can let go of revenge fantasies, cease any and all attempts to make life difficult (let alone dangerous) for your ex-spouse; if you can bring yourself to hope with at least passable sincerity that he or she achieves happiness and success, along with the mental health he or she heretofore so obviously lacked... then I for one will think you've done pretty well.

Where do divorced couples get the idea that they should be friends?

I supposed there is an understandable unwillingness to be deprived of the good parts of the connection, and of course, it probably also comes from a sincere desire to avoid the deleterious effects of divorce on children. If a child's parents have to tell her they don't love each other anymore, perhaps it would salve her sorrow and calm her fears if they claim with some sincerity to *like* each other?

In a cynical mood, I could point out that if a departing spouse would just as soon not suffer through the anger, pain, and the various other unfriendly feelings that an involuntary ex might naturally wish to express, it would be convenient indeed to be able to cite a cultural expectation or norm of friendship. After all, it does happen, if rarely.

I might humbly suggest, however, that the expectation is also the result of a misunderstanding of the character of *caritas*, of love. As Woolie's classmate Olive discerned, love doesn't require us to be friends with everyone. Love really has just that one absolute, implacable demand, and to *desire the achievement of wholeness by the beloved* is not the same as being able to assist in that achievement, let alone impose it. So if Jesse's wife, Georgina, is indeed "deluded and manipulative," Jesse can't fix her. If Jesse is "boring and emotionally warped," as Georgina would have it, Georgina may not be capable of curing him or straightening him out. Sometimes the best we can do is to step aside and allow a more qualified person to be the friend, the healer, the moral chiropractor, while we turn our attention to those who can make better use of the gifts we have to offer.

To want your children to achieve wholeness is—or perhaps should be—the earnest desire of any parent. It is certainly my earnest desire. I want them to be good, honorable, and loving people, and I want my children to remain physically whole—hence the organic grains, limits on television, and use of helmets and other safety devices, not to mention the savage mother-tiger persona that emerges whenever a threat is perceived. Even now, after nearly a decade spent witnessing all kinds of mayhem as a law enforcement chaplain, I can be brought to blithering panic by the sight of my own child's skinned knee.

Simon's athletic daughter, Ilona, wrestled for her middle school wrestling team. In the middle of a match, she broke her collarbone. At the hospital, I asked if I could see the x-ray.

I've always loved the magical glimpse of ghost-bones an x-ray offers. I've seen my own x-rays, including the CAT scan that sliced up my head like salami, and never felt other than fascinated by these. The hospital radiologist obligingly flicked the large film onto the wall-mounted lightbox, and there was Ilona's skeleton, the collarbone looking as frail as the bone of a little bird, snapped in half.

"That's when I knew that Ilona had moved into the part of my heart reserved for persons I consider my own," I told Simon. "I got woozy, and my legs almost trembled right out from under me."

"What kind of mother would let a six-year-old kid ride an ATV alone?" Though Jesse's tone was interrogative, he didn't really require an answer.

An all-terrain vehicle can easily go forty or fifty miles an hour, and there is no restraint and no protection for a rider who can't hold on when the going gets rough, especially if the rider is only six years old.

"Two o'clock in the afternoon, her little girl is out on the ATV with no helmet and no supervision, and the neighbor is the one who found her. When I got there, Mom was still sitting at the kitchen table, drinking coffee brandy, bombed out of her mind. There's an ambulance outside on her front lawn and they're loading her little girl onto a backboard. And Mom hasn't noticed a thing."

"Where was the dad?" I asked.

Jesse exhaled sharply through his nostrils in a sour semblance of a laugh. "Texas or something. He owes her child support, she said. It's in the decree, and the state is trying to *garnish* his wages. That's what she told me: 'His wages gonna git *garnished* if he don' start payin' up!' I wanted to say, 'What kind of garnish are you picturing, lady? Maybe a radish?'" Jesse rubbed his hands wearily over his face.

Nothing matters more than _____. How does the alcoholic mom fill that blank—not just with what word but with what act, what kind of life? How does the deadbeat dad answer? *Nothing matters more than coffee brandy/my hangover/my loneliness/my boredom. Nothing matters more than my illusions…* Maybe any word other than *love* that a person might put in that blank will translate, in the end, to this: *Nothing matters more than me.*

Oh, and who knows what they had to work with, Mom and Dad—who knows what unlucky dearth of affection or education or wholesome genes lies behind their failure to protect? And now that there is injury, should we really expect a parent to shape up, stand tall, and be responsible for what she had failed to be responsible for up to this point: her child's well-being, her own child's life?

Sometime it happens. Sometimes a shock comes along and startles us into seeing what we should have seen and doing what we should have been doing all along. Sometimes a window opens: I know this, and I know it is grace, undeserved, when it happens.

This time, a little child lay badly injured on a hospital gurney while her mother paced up and down out in the parking lot. Smoking was permitted there, and the angry eyes of the game wardens, the social worker, and the ER nurses couldn't aim themselves at her. Plus she could talk to the warden service chaplain who walked by her side.

"I told 'er not to ride that thing s'fast. Dumb kid."

Chapter Twenty-two

Simon was turning an exquisite little porcelain cup over in his strong hands. The cup was still warm from his kiln. The walls of this vessel were so delicate, they were translucent, the glaze glowing cream and celadon in the light from his studio windows. "Do you know why Japanese cups are made without handles?" he asked me. "If the cup is too hot to hold, the tea will be too hot to drink."

He said it matter-of-factly, with no particular emphasis in his voice, but the man is a teacher. "My rabbi," I called him, among other endearments. I wrote this remark in my journal and I still quote it to myself as an explanatory metaphor for anything requiring patience, from my children's teenaged angst to the angry disbelief of a warden whose heart is crushed.

"I'm being civilized," Jesse announced.

"Are you?"

"Yes. She finally fessed up."

"She…Georgina?"

"Yep. About Mr. Right. Or at least, Mr. Better-Than-Me."

"Oh, Jesse."

"Yep. Sucks."

We were quiet for a time, allowing the revelation to settle.

"Do you know him?"

"He was a year behind me in high school. Funny, she'd been telling me it wasn't about other guys, that she's all done with guys, she hates men, she's happiest on her own, wants to be her own woman. Guess not, but then, dude isn't much of a man."

"Oh, Jesse…" I said again, uselessly.

"Well, he's not a *cop,* anyway. Scrawny little feller with a soul-patch beard. She says she is definitely and absolutely all done with law enforcement. I wanted to tell her: 'Baby, you are nowhere near done with law enforcement.' I mean, you should see this guy's 10-27, Kate. Phil Gerard—you know him? trooper up around Danville?—Phil pinched him two years ago for OUI. I guess he still doesn't have his license back, so Georgie-girl is doing all the driving." Jesse gave forth with another laugh: It sounded slightly shrill.

"I'm so sorry."

"Don't be sorry! It's all about being civilized. So I said, 'Georgina, baby, it's all good. In fact, it's *better* than good. It's perfect. I've decided you are totally right. You and I do not belong together, Georgina. Our relationship was doomed from jump-street, baby, a mistake top down and bottom up! You tried to tell me we had nothing in common, absolutely nothing, and at last, hallelujah, I believe! I am convinced, heart and mind, that you and Clark (dude's name is Clark) are absolutely, utterly, entirely right for each other. Never, *never* in all the long history of human pair-bonding has so perfect and precise a match been made between a male and a female of our species than you and Mr. O.U.I. Clark." Jesse smiled beatifically.

"Ouch," I said.

"Yep. Civilized."

"Did you really say all that?'

"Well, no," Jesse said, and squeaked out another laugh. "I just started bawling. Not as civilized."

"But more human," I said.

June rain: Sleek rods rather than droplets were coming from the sky, striking the ground so hard that the bouncing water created the illusion of a solid mass hovering a foot above the grass. Woolie and Ilona—our scrawny girls—came into the living room, pleading: Might they please, please go out and run around naked in the rain?

"Of course," said Simon.

"Underpants," I said.

So I nestled next to him, curled against his warm chest, my head tucked under his jaw and his strong arms around me, and we listened to the music of the day: wild, drum-

ming rain and shrilly fluting girls running through it in their
brightly colored underpants.

In the Gospel of Matthew, a rich young man comes to Jesus,
seeking the secret of salvation. He is not satisfied by Jesus'
reiteration of the commandments: "I have kept all these," the
rich young man says. "What do I still lack?"

Jesus answers, "Go, sell your possessions and give the
money to the poor, and you will have treasures in heaven.
Then come and follow me." It breaks the rich man's heart,
but he can't bring himself to give up what he has (Matthew
19:16–22).

This story can be interpreted, with considerable justice,
to mean that wealth is a spiritual disability in itself. Indeed,
after the rich young man departs, Jesus makes that famous
crack about how the rich get into heaven the way a camel
passes through the eye of a needle: With difficulty, that is, if
at all.

There is another way of thinking about it, though. This
can be a story about attachment and detachment. Like the
young man in the story, I would once have told Jesus, "Look,
buddy. I'm a good person. I don't cheat on my husband, or
put poison in the oatmeal of my enemies; I'm pretty decent
to my parents, all things considered. I keep the commandments. What else is there?"

Jesus might have answered: "What can you not bear to
lose?"

This moment: *My daughters, flying around the wet garden on their absurdly, long flamingo legs...*

The next day, I was sitting on a massive granite slab, part of a retaining wall beside a culvert that channels an inland stream into the top end of Machias Harbor. I was thinking about Woolie and Ilona, Jesse, and the inevitability of loss. I suppose my skin was technically dry inside my rain pants and under my slicker, but I had been standing or sitting around in the rain all day, and the last time the warden diver Bruce Loring climbed out of the water to change out his gear, he had suggested that I might actually stay drier if I jumped into the harbor with him.

Of course I could have gone to sit in the dive trailer and allow my clothes and skin to truly dry. It would have been warmer, and my fingertips could have depruned themselves. I could have eaten my Salvation Army lunch—Dinty Moore beef stew!—undiluted. Instead I was sitting out here, with water at my feet and water pouring down on my head from the sky, and I was pretending it was a zen exercise. In reality, I was attached to a certain outcome: I wanted to be present if and when the divers found the body they were looking for: a drunk driver whose empty car had been discovered up-current from this site. Plus—I can identify this attachment too—there's a quasi-maternal desire to count the heads of the divers as they surface, to offer a bunch of grown men the illusory protection of my mama-gaze. Ah, well.

*   *   *

After a while, sensing a presence, I turned my head, push-ing the stiff edge of my raincoat's hood back from my face. It was an old man, the one who had come out onto his front porch across the road from the harbor around lunchtime to watch the dive team work. Evidently, he wanted a closer look, because he had come across the road and down onto the wet rocks, where he now stood beside me. I smiled up at him and said hello. He nodded.

I wiped my nose with my sleeve and introduced myself. "How are you doing today?" I asked him. He twitched his shoulder in the faint semblance of a shrug.

"Can't complain."

The old man and I spent a quarter hour in silence, watch-ing the divers' black heads emerge and resubmerge (*one... two... three...*) beneath the rain-battered surface of the water. The water was a thick brown broth churned by the current, by tide and rain, and the divers groped through it. (Bruce told me he was just hoping he would find the body with his gloved hand rather than, say, with his face.)

Pulling my hood down onto my wet shoulders—it was really just channeling water down my back anyway—I made another try at conversation.

"Some weather!" I said.

The old man nodded and then, apparently feeling that politeness demanded more, said, "Yuh."

"Do you think the rain will stop?"

The old man shrugged. "Always does," he said.

*   *   *

That night, driving home with the heat blowing hard and music on the radio, I chuckled again at this. I was happy, anyway: The body was retrieved; the victim's family could stop hoping and move along to grief. "My" divers were well and satisfied with the day's work, headed safely home to those they loved.

Do you think this rain will stop?

Always does.

Again I laughed, and shook my head. I was safely headed home to the one I loved too. I was headed home to Simon.

Chapter Twenty-three

Given the ubiquity of sexual pair-bonds that are found, with only minor variations, throughout human cultures and human history, I could probably make the case that monogamous marriage is natural—or at least as natural as anything else human beings do. However, I would question the common notion that happiness will be the inevitable result of compliance with nature's ideal, whatever that turns out to be.

Neither the God of the Bible nor nature would seem to place an especially high priority on human contentment. As the science writer Robert Wright put it (in *The Moral Animal*), "Natural selection never promised us a rose garden. It doesn't 'want' us to be happy. It 'wants' us to be genetically prolific" (211). Similarly, God does not offer his servant Abraham, let alone Abraham's poor old wife, Sarah, a personally fulfilling or even pain-free life. God promises instead that they shall have descendants as numerous as stars.

Abraham and Sarah were more or less monogamous, relatively faithful. Yeah, they had their two-timing moments: Sarah spent some time in Pharoah's harem; Abraham had his wife-approved reproductive interlude with Hagar. These caused discomfort for the various participants in ways any twenty-first-century adult might recognize. Still, their joined story ended the way the good ones do: "Sarah died at Kiriath-naan (that is, Hebron) in the land of Canaan; and Abraham went in to mourn for Sarah and to weep for her" (Genesis 23:2).

So, Kate-O! I imagine God inquiring. *Why not consider Simon, the man who bronzes, yes, and who fixes things but whose hands are warm and strong, and who somehow understands you more deeply than the time you've spent together should allow? What's the matter?* God asks. *Are ya chicken?*

Um...yeah.

Simon confessed to being a little scared too.

"The word *wife* doesn't have good associations for me," he said.

"Interesting," I said. "I can't bring myself to call you my *boyfriend,* but the word *husband* sounds okay."

We drag our old pain, our old fear around with us, don't we? You'll remember when I was on the island with the children—that island where Ellie and Woolie were abandoned by their brothers, lost, then found? Well, I was in the tiny kitchen of the island cottage, making scrambled eggs and probably thinking grateful thoughts about the paramedic

Joel while I whisked the eggs and poured them into the buttered pan I'd set on the front burner of the old two-burner stove. I found a cheap metal fork in a drawer and began to stir the eggs around in the pan.

Then, very suddenly, the whole right side of my body went numb. My right arm began to twitch and tingle in a very unpleasant way. *Parasthesia!* I thought instantly. *My nervous system is malfunctioning! It's multiple sclerosis... that doctor was right after all. I really do have MS... and now my poor children, orphans already, will have a paraplegic mother...*

Oddly enough, though my hand was trembling, I kept doggedly stirring those eggs. It was as if one part of my brain could register a crisis while the other stayed firmly in denial, focused on making lunch. *How will they manage? Will I be incontinent? Will our health insurance cover a home health nurse? Are the doorways in my house wide enough to accommodate a wheelchair?* I stirred and stirred the eggs. At last a rational voice, asserting itself from some small, squashed corner of my mind, managed to get a thought in edgewise: *Kate*, it said. *There is a short in the stove. You are being electrocuted. Drop the fork, and you will be okay.*

So I did. And I was.

I've been married. Simon has also been married. He divorced and, as his son, Cobus, would later inform the crowd at our rehearsal dinner, went on to date "all the beautiful single women in Midcoast Maine." ("He makes it sound like I'm a disease risk," said Simon, sotto voce.) Between us, Simon and

I have six children: three boys and three girls between the ages of fourteen and twenty. "We don't just have baggage," says Simon. "We've got *biomass.*"

If we both had baggage, history, fear, and faults to confess, Simon and I also had—each—a house and furniture, a substantial quantity of books, artwork we had chosen on the walls. We had our own careers, children, hobbies, bank accounts, credit cards.

Incredibly, though we had lived for years in the same small community, we had our own social circles, although when we got around to comparing notes, it was clear that there was considerable overlap between these. We were well established, full grown. We did not require completion.

"I was only able to do it," Simon would later say, of marrying me, "because I didn't need to."

Oh, but there would be need. I knew I would come to depend on the clasp of his strong, warm hand as if it were food, to yearn for the familiar scent of his hair. To say yes to each other would be to create a bond as bone-deep as any monastic vow. I knew enough to be scared. And I was.

"In the sight of God and these beloved witnesses, Jeremy and Melanie have pledged themselves to each other as husband and wife. Therefore, by the power vested in me by the State of Maine, I pronounce that they are married.

"Jeremy...Melanie...you may kiss your wife...and you may kiss your husband...for the first time."

They kissed with passion as fierce as the grave, and all

around them laughter, applause, music. So I removed my clerical collar, had a beer, and danced. Warden Gillespie introduced his chaplain to his daughter, Molly. Georgina was there as well. She stood next to me while we watched Jeremy and Melanie cut the cake and feed each other.

"I'm glad they didn't mash it in each other's faces," she said as I handed her a paper plate of wedding cake and a fork. She looked, suddenly, very young, maybe even as young as I once was.

"Me too," I said.

"We're trying to make things right," she whispered earnestly. "Jesse and me, I mean."

"I know you are," I said. "It's hard."

The following week, Simon and I were invited to the wedding of Monty and Alan at their home in Lincolnville Beach. Alan's nine-year-old niece delivered First Corinthians with unusual brio; Monty's old roommate from Philly read Neruda's "Love Sonnet XVII"... and got as far as "I love you as certain dark things are to be loved, in secret between the shadow and the soul" before she choked up. A woman in a flowered dress and a big hat trilled Pachabel on an electric organ, the mothers dabbed at their eyes with Kleenex, and a couple of errant nephews launched a stealthy, premature assault on the wedding cake.

"I feel," Simon said as we walked home from the wedding, "as though I am, at last, pretty firmly planted." He made vertical lines with his hands in front of us, as though drawing the trunk of a stout oak in the air. "And I am learning to open my arms more and more"—he spread his powerful arms to the sides—"so I can embrace more and love more."

Oh! I said. And turned in to his arms. "If Alan and Monty are brave enough to marry," Simon said as he held me, "who are we to shy away?"

Chapter Twenty-four

Teacher," a lawyer asks Jesus, "which commandment in the law is the greatest?" Jesus answers: "You shall love the Lord your God with all your heart, and with all your soul and with all your mind. This is the greatest and first commandment. And a second is like unto it: You shall love your neighbor as yourself. There is no other commandment greater than these" (Matthew 22:34–40, Mark 12:28–34, Luke 10: 25–28).

If a person can begin by loving God and proceed to love her neighbor, bully for her. I had to start with loving Drew within the cloister of our union, wherein each of us could indeed be master and slave, rabbi and disciple, answer and question, window and...Windex?

From there, I could expand my own capacity for love the way a glassblower expands a vessel's molten walls.

"Breath by breath," as Simon would say. "It's all done breath by breath, Kate-O."

Maybe we will eventually come up with a more rational arrangement for organizing family life than centering it on a sexual pair-bond, something just as useful but less confining. Someday we may discover a better way, but we haven't done it yet. Marriage stubbornly continues to present itself, surfacing like a palimpsest from our boldest attempts to create something better.

Perhaps the clearest and most touching evidence of this has been the demand on the part of gay and lesbian couples that they too be able to publicly and legally name their unions *marriage:* Okay, maybe Monty and Alan are just as deluded as everyone else. Their delusions, however moving I might find them, provide the cynic with no reason to renounce pessimism when it comes to this tattered and tottering institution.

One can easily use the fact of antimiscegenation laws to demonstrate how bigoted and evil white southerners were, but it can also reveal the opposite: that even in the American South, after years of slavery, Jim Crow, violence, and relentless racist propaganda, a black person and a white person might do exactly what Alvin and Omelia Gardner did down in North Carolina back in 1968. They met, they fell in love, and decided to spend the rest of their days together. Wedded just as soon as the Supreme Court said they could, the Gardners have now been married for more than forty years. In their quite normal, ordinary, and particular human union is revealed the inherently subversive, unquenchable, and ultimately ungovernable power of human bonding and human love.

Because human love and Holy Love are inextricably bound together, any human love has the capacity to teach us *caritas*, any human love story is both ordinary and Holy, life becoming myth as it is lived and told breath by breath.

The first time I purchased a wedding dress, my mother and I were forced to consult Mom's stylish friend Sandy, and even she could only persuade us to go to one store. Wisely, Sandy selected a shop with just three dress models to choose from. I chose one. Mom paid for it. We went to the bookstore.

There's a good bookstore right next door to the Black Parrot Boutique in Rockland, Maine, but the stated purpose of this day's expedition was to find and purchase wedding-wear, not just for me but for all of the female members of the soon-to-be family.

Woolie had forgotten this. She was over in the shoe section, ogling a pair of sleek black leather boots. They were very cool, but hardly appropriate for summer nuptials. Her sister, Ellie, meanwhile, had found a dress she might be willing to wear, but a smidgeon of dust in the dressing room triggered her asthma and gave her a nosebleed. So she was standing over by the door, a Kleenex pressed to her upper lip, patiently waiting for this ordeal to be over.

Like Ellie, I detest a fitting room. I was sympathetic to

Woolie's distraction. Dutifully examining a selection of spangled confections, I was longing to declare defeat and run away. But my soon-to-be stepdaughter, Ilona, was rummaging enthusiastically through the sale rack, surveying the prospects with an expert's eye. "Ah, *sweet!*" she exclaimed triumphantly. "Now, *this* is a wedding dress!" She held it up for inspection. "And it's half-price."

"I don't know, honey," I said. "It's kind of...revealing."

"Revealing?" scoffed Ilona. "Look how wide these straps are."

"It would show my arms," I explained. "What if my triceps wobble?"

Ilona rolled her eyes and pushed me into the dressing room. When I emerged, swathed in layers of tulle and champagne silk, all three girls gasped.

"Wow. That is *so bad*," said Woolie approvingly.

"You look like a princess," said Ellie.

I surveyed myself critically in a full-length glass. "I look like the Queen Mum," I said.

"You look fantastic," said Ilona smugly. "And my dad is going to love it."

At twenty-three I was willing to imagine that God or fate had deliberately brought Drew into my life, that it had pleased God to unite us. I was sure that long-ago homeless man had been a prophet, pausing in his shambling sojourn to add a strange, holy harmony to my cry: *Hey! I love you too!*

This was the egoism of a young and unbroken heart. No

loss made room for that first union; no excruciating prior endings were required, no deaths. I am humbler now and can no longer imagine that a fine and lucky thing, however welcome, was inevitable. Simon and his first wife did not have to struggle and suffer and be rent apart; Drew did not have to die; I could as easily have caught Simon's eye at a young friend's wedding as at a young friend's funeral. It didn't have to happen the way it did, but this is how it happened. You can ask why, but no matter how the passing prophet gives it voice, the answer will be love. As much as you can, as long as you can: Just love.

"Will you marry me?" Simon asked. He was actually down on one knee, and had a ring to slip on my finger.

"It's beautiful!"

"It's wax," he said. "I've ordered the gold to cast the real thing, but it hasn't arrived yet. Still, I've already called the caterer, so I figured I'd better hurry up and ask. So, will you?"

Did I mention that Simon designed and made my engagement ring? After ponying up the gold one a week or so after giving me the wax model, he would go on to make our wedding rings. He designed and built our house. I may be middle-aged, and a little banged up, emotionally speaking, but I'm not stupid. I said yes.

"In our maturity, we have learned to accept a paradox," Simon said to me later. "We have lost. Now we love and we are grateful."

* * *

Our middle-aged friends count many struggles and failures, wounds healed and unhealed, near losses and losses. You would think our wedding would therefore be attended by pewfuls of cynics, rolling their eyes and muttering sourly under their breath.

Life is short, and pain engraves its memories in your flesh. When the end is near—as the truck comes at me, as my heart discards its rhythm, or as I am falling from an airplane, tumbling and turning in the sky—I suppose my very last thought might be: *It's MS!*

But I hope not.

I hope, instead, that I remember my father, sobbing with mirth beside a Danish highway, or the way an orange sweater glows against my nephew Bagna's skin. I hope I think of Woolie marching over the grassy, blond bluff with the sea behind her and an absolute confidence that love will always be there when it's needed.

"Do you promise to love and honor until you are parted by death?" the minister asked. Standing before ecstatic pewfuls of our friends, swathed in champagne-colored silk, surrounded by our sweet and vulnerable children, with the wisdom, humility, passion, and the lunatic courage of our years, Simon and I promised. Then he kissed his wife and I kissed my husband, for the first time.

POSTLUDE

When I was a new widow, my kindly cousin Tommy, wishing to cheer me up, decided to take me to see a taping of *Saturday Night Live* in New York. *Saturday Night Live* is broadcast in the middle of the night, so I had to stay up well past my normal bedtime, and—wouldn't you know it?—it had been one of the bad days, anyway. I had been crying continuously for something like fourteen hours when the time came for us to head downtown to the NBC studio. Bundling me into a taxi, Tommy was clearly uneasy at the prospect of escorting this soggy, woeful cousin anyplace others might see us.

"Tom-my...don't...don't worry about me-e-e-eeeee!" I snuffled.

"You'll be fine," Tommy said in an attempt at bracing cheer. "You'll shape up when we get to the studio."

I gave a tremendous snort and (this was unattractive) swallowed. "You know what my dad always told me?" I offered in a quavering voice.

"What's that?" said Tommy.

Having a quantity of mucus in my throat made it easier to imitate my father's voice: "'Kate-O,' he'd say. 'Kate-O, if an experience is good, it's good. If the experience is bad, it will make a *terrific* story!'"

My father was Tommy's Uncle Peter. Tommy grinned.

"So I'm thinking that if, you know... if going to see *Saturday Night Live* cheers me up, that will be a good thing... but if I cry through the whole show, won't it make a great story?"

I'm not sure Tommy was as comforted by this idea as I was.

In any case, that night Tommy and I happened to be part of the audience for the mayor and future presidential candidate Rudy Guiliani's comic debut. He appeared in a skit as an old Italian lady in a flowered dress. Sarah McLaughlin was the musical guest. In the end, *Saturday Night Live* cheered me up. Tommy and I had no great story to tell, which was just fine with both of us.

I was thinking about Dad's maxim when it comes to love: When everything goes well, there is no story. Literally the best news I can offer about Simon and me at this moment is that there is no news. Just joy.

Dear Jeremy and dear Melanie:
Congratulations, the beautiful two of you. Don't
worry: You are crazy to marry, but you aren't stupid.
You have each chosen well. May your marriage be
blessed and a blessing, may it grant you joy

commensurate ... nay, disproportionate to *life's inevitable sorrow.*

If you should happen to find yourselves, decades hence, in some ordinary moment, noticing that you are still in love with each other, I hope you will remember the day of your wedding. Let the shadows flee, let that miraculous moment breathe, let the joy rise in you like flowers of flame from the sacred earth on which you stand.

Love and kisses from
your chaplain,
Kate

ACKNOWLEDGMENTS

In writing this book, I describe the lives and relationships of a number of people. As always, the names and other identifying details from various incidents involving civilians have been altered to protect their privacy.

In my last book, *Here If You Need Me,* I took a great deal of time and trouble to change the names of the game wardens I was describing, on the assumption that this would be the general preference, only to be asked, after the fact, "How come you didn't use my name?"

So all right: This time I've used the real names of all game wardens I discuss, with one exception. Readers should know that I have altered not only the names but other details to such an extent that I suppose one could argue that Jesse and Georgina Gillespie are virtually fictional characters. Anyone who recognizes himself or herself in their story is, I would respectfully suggest, identifying universals. We are not, after all, unlike in our joys and our miseries.

Jeremy and Melanie Judd graciously agreed to appear as themselves in this book: I thank them, and all the game wardens, named and unnamed.

I would also like to extend long-overdue thanks to my marvelous agent, Sally Wofford-Girand, and to the fine women and men at Little, Brown who, with generosity, good humor, and consummate professionalism, manage to take my words and make them into real books. Last Christmas, in a not-uncharacteristic frenzy of pre-holiday creativity, I knit ludicrous hats for all of Little, Brown's staff members who work with me: I hope Reagan, Michael, David, Michelle, Luisa, Heather, Mario, and Oliver know that every stitch was made in gratitude, not only for all you have accomplished on behalf of my work, but for your willingness to be moved by the wonders that so move me: the natural beauty of Maine, the courage and compassion of the men and women of the Maine Warden Service, and the extraordinary grace made manifest in ordinary lives.

BACK BAY · READERS' PICK

READING GROUP GUIDE

MARRIAGE

and

OTHER ACTS

of

CHARITY

A memoir by

KATE BRAESTRUP

Kate Braestrup

answers some of the questions she's frequently asked by readers of

Marriage and Other Acts of Charity

1. Do you have any concrete advice for married persons as to how we are supposed to demonstrate love—agape—to a spouse?

Yes. But you might not like it.

The principle I arrived at, after oh! so many struggles, goes like this: My husband is a good, sane, moral man. Not a perfect man, perhaps, but a good man. Not only do I love him, but I trust and admire him. Therefore, *he can have anything he wants from me.* If it is mine to give, all he has to do is ask.

When I declare this, most people seem to respond with an almost comical expression of guarded skepticism. *"Anything?"* someone is sure to enquire, making sure.

Anything.

"Well . . . like what?" my interrogator demands, and I am always tempted to ask what dreadful spousal demand he or she has in mind. Your left arm? The contents of your bank account? Weird sex?

The best example I can offer is this: A couple of years ago, my husband Simon asked me what he might give me for Christmas. My answer was unexpected and, frankly, unwelcome.

"You know that intersection on Route 235?" I said. "The one where the speed limit drops to twenty-five, because the road coming in from the right isn't visible until you're right on it?"

"Yeah . . . ," said Simon, in a voice filled with foreboding.

"For Christmas, I would like for you to always go the speed limit whenever you drive through that intersection. It scares me to think of you getting into an accident right there, because you usually drive through it too fast."

"I don't . . . ," Simon began, and then stopped. "You know, I might just decide to go the other way to Camden for the whole year, and skip that intersection altogether."

"I know," I said. "And that would be fine, too."

Simon could have taken this as an attempt to control him, or as my attempt to make my neurotic worry into his burden. He could have laughed it off, or ridiculed me. Instead, because he knows me to be a good, sane, moral person, someone he admires and trusts as well as loves, he gave me what I wanted. The gift itself (not having to worry that he would be killed in a car accident going through that intersection) and the fact that he was willing to give it to me made this into one of the best Christmas presents I've ever had.

2. Well, and if you give unconditional love to your spouse, they'll give it back to you. Right?

Not necessarily. What made my own experience (and thus my argument) into a religious experience was the revelation that love must be given simply because it's love. There is no quid pro quo, no actual or implied demand for reciprocity along the lines of: "If I give you 'slowing down at the intersection' for Christmas, you've got to give me 'not chewing ice' in return." It's not that there isn't room for this kind of negotiation in marriage (or any other relationship), only that a negotiated settlement isn't a gift. It's not *caritas*. Offering *caritas*, or unconditional love, to someone makes it somewhat more likely that they will do the same . . . but if you think of it that way, you'll end up quantifying something that cannot and should not be quantified. ("I gave you unconditional love 16 percent more often than you gave me unconditional love. . . . Buddy, you owe me!")

Further, we are called to offer our love to all kinds of people who are never going to be in a position to pay us back, even if they wanted to. The expectation, let alone the demand, for recompense is actually anti-love.

So the harsh lesson remains: Why love? Because you can love. Amen.

3. What if your spouse asks you for permission to sleep with someone else?

Emotional reaction first: I would punch him in the snoot.

Spiritual/religious reaction: Strange as it may sound, the vows we make at a wedding are not ultimately about our relationship with the person we are marrying. They are about our relationship with God (however you want to interpret that).

My spouse doesn't need *my* permission to cheat. He needs *God's* permission to cheat—that it is okay to violate a promise made knowingly and in all good conscience, and that this violation (the breaking of a commandment, remember) will not define him as cheater, liar, adulterer.

For the same reason, I can't give my husband permission to murder me or steal from me. I can't tell my neighbor that it's all right with me if he enslaves me or dehumanizes me. Nor may I tell my children they can go ahead and dishonor me. These are not my gifts (if they are gifts) to offer. It's an important distinction.

Let me illustrate it this way: The commandment says, quite clearly, *thou shall not kill*. I work with police officers who, as part of their commitment to the public's protection, are put in a position where they might have to break that commandment. But ultimately it isn't the government, or the American public, or the chaplain who can give them permission to kill, nor can any of us grant them absolution afterward. Only love— as motivation, as intention, as character, as response—can declare that this officer, though he has killed, is not a killer.

4. *What about abusive spouses?*

My husband is not an abusive spouse. If he were an abusive spouse, the best possible gift I could give to myself, my children, his future relationships (if any), *and to him* would be to refuse to allow him to abuse me. This is the only gift I can give to anyone who would hurt me: I can't reform him/her or fix him/her, I can't make him/her into the person he or she might be and may even want to be. The only contribution I am capable of making to the healing of the abuser, the mugger, the rapist, the bigot, the terrorist, or the dictator is my resistance to victimhood, and my attempt to protect other potential victims.

5. *What is your opinion about gay marriage?*

My opinion of gay marriage is exactly the same as my opinion of straight marriage: It's impossibly difficult and sure to end in agony. So I say: "No more of this uncommitted fiddling around! Everyone should grow up and git hitched."

Questions and Topics

FOR DISCUSSION

1. What is the source of the tensions in Kate Braestrup's first marriage? How does her view of the discord differ from that of her husband?

2. What, in Braestrup's opinion, can a good marriage provide? How is this different from what you expect marriage to give you?

3. Braestrup mentions several times that she helped people who had been placed in her path. What does it mean to help those who have been placed in your path? Why do you think Kate and the taxi driver help the injured woman who makes racist remarks (page 16)?

4. Can it be argued, as Braestrup claims, that "our society has moved beyond the stage of requiring the sort of social cohesion that religious practice is capable of producing" (page 68)? Discuss the role of religion in your life, and in the lives of your family members or your friends.

5. How is the definition of *caritas,* or love, different from our modern conception of love? Do you think that love is selfish or selfless?

6. Why does Braestrup change her thinking from "Why me?" to "Why not me?" when she is misdiagnosed for multiple sclerosis? How does her thinking change when she is introduced to her nephew, Bagna, or when she learns she is, in fact, healthy?

7. What does Oscar mean when he says that Jesus is the window, rather than the view? What do you think it means to "worship the pane" rather than the view (page 102)?

8. What does it mean to earnestly desire the achievement of wholeness? Have you ever felt this way toward someone?

9. Braestrup claims that all relationships end, and asks us to consider: What are we to do in the face of loss (page 137)? Discuss how you have dealt with loss in the past and how you might deal with it in the future.

10. Why is Kate Braestrup's advice for a broken heart to love even more? Does this make sense to you?

11. Braestrup tells Woolie's class that they should fill in the blank for the following sentence: "*NOTHING MATTERS MORE THAN* _____" (page 156). She then tells the students that however they answer the question, it will be their working definition of God. How would you fill in the blank? Do you think this is an acceptable definition of God?

12. Discuss the book's title. In what ways might marriage constitute an act of charity?

About the Author

Kate Braestrup is the chaplain for the Maine Warden Service. She is the author of two other works of nonfiction—*Here If You Need Me,* a memoir, and *Beginner's Grace: Bringing Prayer to Life*—and of the novel *Onion.* She has written for the *New York Times Magazine;* the *Boston Globe Sunday Magazine;* O, *The Oprah Magazine; Mademoiselle; More;* and *Ms.* She lives in Maine with her husband and children.

Following is an excerpt from the opening pages of *Here If You Need Me.*

With perhaps another fifteen years to go before he could retire from his job as a trooper for the Maine State Police, my husband James Andrew "Drew" Griffith was already planning a second career as a Unitarian Universalist minister. He imagined himself serving a church and working as a law enforcement chaplain on the side. He could respond to crime scenes and search scenes, perform death notifications, and help families and officers cope with the spiritual and emotional dimensions of the work he was all too familiar with in his current occupation. Earnest, intelligent, brave, and tender, Drew would have made a great minister.

According to our plan, I would have gone on writing, but I would also be a minister's wife. It would have been a fine life.

One Monday morning in April 1996, my alarm clock went off. My husband grunted, turned over, and reached for me.

For a half hour we snoozed entwined, a caduceus of warm, familiar flesh, until the backup alarm clock on his side of the bed rang, the dogs appeared at the bedside, and a child began to stir in the next room.

Two hours after this, the sheets were still tangled and, doubtless, still held the residual heat of his body as well as his scent. Downstairs, where I stood in the kitchen, Drew's cereal bowl was in the sink. White bowl, stainless steel sink. My husband's body, at that moment, lay along the front seat of his cruiser, his crew-cut head resting gently in the crook of his arm, just as if, his friend Tom would later tell me, he had decided to take a nap there, in the lemon-colored sunlight of an April morning.

"I don't know," the sergeant said, when I asked to be taken to the scene to see the body.

In the local paper that very afternoon, there would be photographs showing the smashed Maine State Police cruiser and the back end of a paramedic protruding from the passenger-side door. The front end of the paramedic—Peter Lammert, I know him—was trying to determine what, if anything, could be done to hold my husband's life in his body. There was nothing. The impact of a fully loaded box truck striking the driver's side of a car carries a force that neither the car door nor the body behind it is designed to withstand. By any ordinary measure, Drew died instantly.

Death can be plausibly described as instantaneous, yet our

cells have a certain autonomy. Only when the heart is stilled and the blood no longer streams effervescent with oxygen do the cells begin to shut down. It can take a while—six hours or more—for the last cellular outposts to flicker into darkness.

For hours, and only a mile or so from home, Drew's body lay on the driver's seat of his cruiser. One by one, or perhaps in clusters, his cells extinguished themselves. Finally, the driver's side door was cut away from where it held him in a grip both tenacious and tender. The crumpled metal did not bruise him; a little blood showed at the corner of his mouth, but nowhere else, I was told. He was loaded into a hearse and driven to the state medical examiner's lab in Augusta—and by that time it was at last accurate, even on the level of the microscopic, to refer to what was loaded as an "it" and not a "him."

I would go to the bridge only days later. There were skid marks on its asphalt surface. They began precisely where the truck collided with the car. They marked an instant in time as a point in space. When no cars were passing by, it was possible to hear the river, the moving air, the birds. It was possible to stand or place a hand or sink to my knees on that place—amid the fragments of red and clear glass, the flecks of smoky blue paint, the bits of metal—where my husband's life came to an end.

Love begins with the body; the love between Drew and me certainly did, in any case. He was very handsome, although I didn't think so when we first met. He was a photographer then, not yet a police officer. He had a scraggly beard and longish hair. He exercised assiduously, which did not endear him to me. I fancied myself an intellectual at twenty-one and believed attention to one's physique smacked of narcissism. Though riven by the same, stupid combination of vanity and anxiety that most young women are prey to, I pretended an enlightened disinterest in the whole culture of physical perfection. I did not shave my legs. I chopped off my own hair. For Drew's well-developed forearms, ridged abdomen, and the impressive spread of his latissimus dorsi, I had only condescension. In theory, anyway. But when he called to ask if I'd like to see a movie with him, I said yes. This could be described as mere lust, and lust was involved, of course. But *lust* is too diffuse: it will attach itself to punk-rock drummers and English professors and wholly imaginary persons. Its real power is only acquired through specificity: I want not a body, but *this* body, this one here, Drew's body, his scent and heat, his scary strength, his warm mouth.

Once he became a state trooper, Drew's professional life had an intimate physical aspect. He had to do brave and loving things to and with the bodies of others. Take, for example, those he arrested, particularly those who fought back, the ones he would have to wrestle with, the weight of his body pressing them into the ground, his mouth against an ear shouting instructions ("Give it up! Give it up!") as he groped beneath a sweaty belly for hands and weapons. Those bodies smelled of inadequate hygiene and, nearly always, of alcohol. When he had them safely handcuffed, he would help them up and cradle the backs of their heads in his palm so they wouldn't hurt themselves getting into his cruiser. Once he took the tiny hand of an abused four-year-old girl who led him out back, behind her house, to show him where her father had chopped her puppy to pieces with an ax. Drew held the shape of that small hand in his palm for weeks. There were the bodies of those who, on receiving official police notification of a loved one's death, collapsed against his Kevlar-stiffened chest and wept. He would hold them gently and murmur, "That's all right. That's all right."

His body was a tool of his trade, trained to the arcane demands of policing: the holds, takedowns, cuff 'n' stuff, and CPR. So he lifted weights, bicycled, and ran long distances— fast. His arms could press a lot of iron away from his chest. His heart was in superb condition: low blood pressure, cholesterol count in the peachy zone. His body became more beautiful with every passing year, something that after our four babies could not be said of mine. "You will always be beautiful to me," he would tell me, kissing me, and maybe I would have.

He heard the book reviewed on National Public Radio, and so, for my thirty-first birthday, my husband gave me a heavy tome entitled *Death to Dust: What Happens to Dead Bodies?*, by Kenneth V. Iserson, MD. I considered this a wildly romantic gift. Who but Drew would know how entranced I would be by such a book? I spent two weeks immersed in its pages, emerging at intervals to engage him in discussions of funereal arcana: organ donation, embalming, postmortem cosmetics, the expense of coffins and urns, cremation, and so on. Iserson's primary ambition for the book was to increase the number of organ donors by enlightening readers to the impossibility of avoiding the "mutilating" effects of death, which, the claims of the funeral industry notwithstanding, are inevitable even in the most thoroughly embalmed corpse. His secondary theme was that the care of a loved one's dead body was, until very recently, an intimate privilege, one now usurped by professionals.

Modern culture does not encourage us, let alone require us, to take care of the bodies of our dead, any more than we are required to take care of our loved ones as they give birth or suffer or die. Instead, we are offered the expensive illusion that through a mortician's skills the bodies of those we love will remain. There will be roses in their cheeks, chemicals in their systems, and thickly padded coffins to preserve those beloved limbs from the saprophytes that would otherwise claim them. Your loved one will never be dirt, they say.

Iserson recommends resisting this illusion. He advocates giving away undamaged organs to the needy living, and caring for what remains personally—bathing the colorless face, arranging the stiffened limbs, choosing a garment, and dressing the corpse. Dig the hole yourself, if you can. Get the dust and ash on your own hands.

After all, for thousands and thousands of years, ordinary people dealt with their own dead. Why is it that we have not evolved to tolerate and, in some sense, to actively require the experience of personally preparing and burying the bodies of those we love? My father, a former Marine, told me that part of the pledge Marines make is that nobody—no body— is left on the field of battle. *Semper fidelis*. Even the dead are retrieved, sometimes at considerable risk to the living. Why bother to make such a pledge, unless it is desirable that our bodies not fall into the hands of loveless strangers, even after our souls have departed?

"Will you take care of my body when I die?" I shouted to Drew from my chair on the lawn, where I read Dr. Iserson's book and nursed our fourth baby under the willow tree. Drew was setting up the sprinkler for the older children to play in.

"Sure, honey," he answered, and I, like a Marine, felt distinctly braver.

When the funeral director, Mr. Moss, arrived early Tuesday morning, I knew precisely what our preferences were when it came to the disposal of what Mr. Moss gently referred to as "the remains."

I am his remains, I thought.

"You may not embalm him," I said. "Not even a little bit. And no makeup, either. He is to be cremated, and I would like to witness the cremation." Mr. Moss had spread pamphlets and a catalog with pictures of coffins across the dining room table. I did not look at them.

At that moment, Drew's body was being autopsied. Tests for systemic drugs and alcohol were performed, and all, unsurprisingly, came back negative. The chest cavity was opened, his lungs and good stout heart examined, the cause of death confirmed: lacerations to the aorta, to the anterior vestibule of the heart, to the superior vena cava—devastating injuries to all major internal organs, which could not be "harvested." The brain was removed, weighed, examined for defects that might have added complexity to the accident investigation. There were none.

"Drew would have wanted the cheapest possible coffin," I told Mr. Moss, "provided it is also the one that will cremate most completely and with the least environmental impact." The cheapest coffin, which was essentially made of cardboard, turned out, by happy coincidence, to be covered with a nice, state-police-blue fabric.

"That's perfect," I said.

"Good," Mr. Moss replied. "And you want to attend the cremation?"

"Yes," I said. "In addition, I want to bathe and dress his body myself. And I will be the one who closes his coffin for the last time."

"You prefer to, ah, do the dressing and so forth to the body *yourself*," Mr. Moss said carefully, making sure.

"Yes," I said. "I do."

Stainless steel sink, a white bowl, and a stainless spoon, bathed in the lemon yellow light of that morning. I picked up the spoon and put it in my mouth. It tasted of steel and milk. I wanted it to be warm. I wanted it to be Drew.

My son Peter came into the kitchen. I reached for him, but he did not come to me right away. "Maybe Dad has been reincarnated already," he said. His voice was raw, fierce. Peter was seven years old. His father had been dead for two hours. "Maybe Dad is a tiger."

"She wants to bathe and dress the body."

"She wants to *what?*"

"She wants to bathe and dress the body."

"Oh, Jesus. Herself?"

The discussion between the funeral director and higher-ups in the state police went on in this vein late into Tuesday evening and on into Wednesday morning.

What were they afraid of? The same thing I was afraid of. The same thing any of us might be afraid of these days, when birth and death are not "processed" in our homes by our own hands. We have no experience to guide us.

I am quite sure that from the outside my desire to see and to care for my husband's body appeared unshakable. Looking back, I can admit to doubts: *What if my beloved's corpse disgusts me? What if seeing him and touching him make it hurt more?* Yet by instinct as well as by a more intellectual conviction, I knew that I had to walk up to that which would hurt me most: Drew's body without Drew in it. I wanted to do it not because it would help me heal—healing was both indefinable and unimaginable—but because it was the authoritative command of an authentic love. Tuesday night, I lay on Drew's pillow, in his smell, and did not sleep. His body would arrive at the funeral parlor the next morning. *How could it possibly hurt more than this?*

Also by Kate Braestrup

Here If You Need Me

A True Story

"A superbly crafted memoir.... The journey of a strong-minded, warmhearted woman through tragedy to grace."
—Jane Ciabattari, *Washington Post*

"Braestrup writes great truths simply and easily."
—Sarah Peasley, *Rocky Mountain News*

"It's not required that you share Braestrup's faith to be moved by her struggle to maintain it. She is not a soul saver or a pulpit pounder. She is merely a fellow searcher—more tenderhearted (and funnier) than most."
—*Time*

"Kate Braestrup's search for her place in the world is an inspiration and a joy."
—Susan Larson, *New Orleans Times-Picayune*

"Kate Braestrup's role as both memoirist and minister is to ponder why bad things happen to good people and, as a grieving widow, to accept that death comes for its own reasons and on its own schedule. This she does affectingly, with style and grace."
—Amanda Heller, *Boston Globe*

Back Bay Books
Available wherever paperbacks are sold